Charles Buchan's
LIVERPOOL
GIFT BOOK

selections from

CHARLES BUCHAN'S PUBLICATIONS

1951-73

Dear Reader,
As this is the first Gift Book which I have edited for you, I would like to begin this little introduction by saying how much I hope you will enjoy the stories and pictures which have been gathered together for you.

I expect many of you who are reading this are already old friends of mine, boys who keep in touch with our greatest game through the columns of "Football Monthly". But, whether we have already met, or whether we are meeting here for the first time, I welcome you all, knowing how keen you are on sport and how sound is your judgement.

Now it is your judgement that can help me. Let me know if you enjoy this book - and if you do like it, tell your pals about it.

If, on the other hand, you have criticisms to make, let me know of them and you can be sure I will do my very best to carry out your suggestions when we publish this book in future years.

The idea has been to give you variety, to provide exciting reading, and to print pictures which will capture highlights of the game and the great footballers who make it so popular with us all.

I believe the recipe will be to your liking and hope that when you have finished this volume you will begin to look forward to next year's!

Charles Buchan's introduction
to his first Soccer Gift Book, 1953–1954

Charles Buchan's Liverpool Gift Book
© Malavan Media and Football Monthly Ltd 2008

Malavan Media is a creative consultancy responsible for the
Played in Britain series of books and events
www.playedinbritain.co.uk

Edited by Simon Inglis
Text by Stephen Done and Simon Inglis
Design by Doug Cheeseman and Jörn Kröger
Production by Jackie Spreckley
Thanks to Simon Gill and Theo Inglis
ISBN: 978 0954744 564
Printed by Zrinski, Croatia

Charles Buchan's

LIVERPOOL
GIFT BOOK

Edited by
Simon Inglis

Introduction by
Stephen Done

Published by Malavan Media

Cont

ents

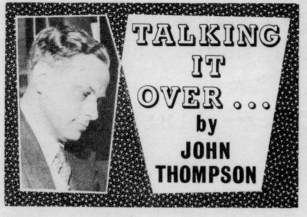

TALKING IT OVER . . . by JOHN THOMPSON

From the beginning . . .

AT first there was one chair in the office of "Football Monthly." I cannot remember why. We were hard-up for furniture for a long time. We would take it in turns to perch round a trestle table on orange boxes and would courteously leave the chair for any visitor who proved himself healthy enough to climb the steep stairs leading to our new home.

The trestle table was covered with a grey blanket and smelled of old apples. This was probably because Covent Garden was just round the corner.

Long before "Football Monthly" increased its tangible assets in any substantial way, Charles Buchan climbed the stairs with a purchase wrapped in brown paper. It was a splendidly **expensive feather-duster.**

Every morning Charles would whisk it energetically over the walls, the little pieces of furniture and the weary strips of linoleum.

Then he would look around as proudly as if he had just scored the winning goal against Scotland.

The moment he had finished, all the dust would settle down gracefully to await the next disturbance. The office overlooked the Strand, London . . . buses almost passed through the room, and it was difficult to keep clean for any time at all.

That first winter was singularly comfortless. In an unenviable spot, furthest from the windows, Joe Sarl would peer with a kind of hopeless determination at typescript and proofs and emerge at the end of the day with the lost look of a man who has been wandering through a thick fog.

He was, however, the warmest of our company.

To avoid frost-bite from the draughts that whistled through the room, Charles Buchan would wrap newspapers round his legs. The paper rustled disconcertingly whenever he moved.

LONG before winter fell, there had been the task of reading the first contributions to our first issue. There had been a fascinating incongruity in sitting on an orange box and studying the earliest article to arrive.

It came from that fine and kindly friend, the Marquess of Londonderry. He had been converted to Soccer by his friendship with miners in his father's pits.

There was a certain dream-like quality in reading Lord Londonderry's description of how he had become a director of Arsenal . . . because of a conversation over dinner at Buckingham Palace with the Master of the Horse, who happened to be Chairman of Arsenal.

Well, Buckingham Palace was only down the road from our office. And for a moment the bare electric light bulb was a candelabrum . . .

As this one hundredth edition of "Football Monthly" was being prepared, I glanced with nostalgia through that long-ago Number One.

The front cover picture was of Stanley Matthews, of Blackpool and England. **There could be no other choice, for Matthews has enriched the pleasures of us all and, in the years that have intervened, there has been no challenger for his place among the giants.**

Inside, were pictures of little Henry Cockburn, of Manchester United, and of Jimmy Dickinson, who has served Portsmouth with devoted loyalty through so many triumphs and disasters.

There, too, were bow-legged Joe Mercer and Mal Griffiths, the happy Welshman, and George Young leading out Scotland, and Jimmy Mason poised over the ball in the colours of Third Lanark. All were players remembered now with gratitude.

There, too, was Joe Harvey, telling with humility of the day Newcastle United won the F.A. Cup . . . *The King handed it to me and as he did so, I had the feeling that all the good people of Tyneside were with me . . . I felt that His Majesty was giving the Cup to me not as Joe Harvey, but as the representative of all those supporters, that I was getting it on their behalf.*

The Queen gave me my medal and I made my way down the steps, perhaps stumbling a little because I was near to tears . . .

TURN again the yellowing pages of that old "Football Monthly". Here is Raich Carter talking of bomb-battered Hull . . . *It was the success of Hull City Soccer team that helped to put Hull back on the map and restore the morale of people who had come to regard themselves as isolated and forgotten . . .*

Arthur Drewry, then Chairman of England's Selectors, told how *his imagination had been fired in Argentina and Brazil by the development of football grounds as first-class social centres; the centre-piece of the local community for every kind of recreative sport . . .*

Turn the pages . . . here is J. B. Priestley, capturing, as he did so well in "The Good Companions", the emotions of those who follow our greatest game . . . *It turned you into a member of a new community, all brothers together for an hour-and-a-half, for not only had you escaped from the clanking machinery of this less life, from work, wages, rent, doles, sick pay, insurance cards, nagging wives, ailing children, bad bosses, idle workmen, but you had escaped with most of your neighbours, with half the town, and there you were, cheering together, thumping one another on the shoulders, swopping judgments like lords of the earth, having pushed your way through a turnstile into another and altogether more splendid kind of life, hurtling with Conflict and yet passionate and beautiful in its Art . . .*

AND now, close the pages and consider for a moment how "Football Monthly" grew from its orange-box days into the voice of the greatest game man ever played, the game that spans frontiers with a handshake and knows no barriers of race or belief.

"Football Monthly" became a unique 'family affair'. Readers sent ideas and views on how to improve the magazine. Never had a publication received such friendly and loyal support.

The family was scattered, as the magic of football is scattered.

There was a boy in Brazil, a shoe-maker in Alaska, a judge's son in Yugoslavia, the skipper of a tug-boat who took two copies so that he could send one to an unknown kid in hospital.

There was a cinema manager in Australia, a cipher clerk in a British Embassy, a lance-corporal in the Malayan jungle.

The addresses from which they wrote ranged from Bolton to Burma. They came from destroyers and trawlers, factories and farms. Some were at village schools, others at Eton.

Thus did "Football Monthly" prosper because of the kindliness and understanding of its readers.

And it is the kindliness that will be remembered always— the gifts that readers asked us to send to sick children at Christmas, the gestures that helped old players down on their luck.

There were letters from prisons and mansions and there was the miracle of finding how blind people retain their love for football.

And the family grew and gained in strength and influence. It is loyal and sturdy, as it always was. We are very proud of it . . .

▲ December 1959

Foreword

by Simon Inglis
Played in Britain series editor

'Our object is to provide a publication that will be worthy of our National game and the grand sportsmen who play and watch it.'

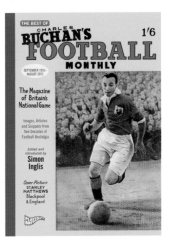

For the discerning football fan of the 1950s and 1960s, *Charles Buchan's Football Monthly* was an absolute essential. If not for reading, then for the supply of bedroom posters.

Of course there were other publications on the market, such as the weekly *Sport* magazine, which ran until 1957, or *Soccer Star*, established in 1952. But neither had such bold design, such vibrant colour images, the collectability, the satisfying weightiness, nor any of the camaraderie that Charles Buchan and his team so knowingly infused into the pages of *Football Monthly*.

To be a reader of Charlie's magazine was to be a member of a fraternity.

In the world of Charles Buchan – a former Sunderland and Arsenal player known to millions for his match reports on BBC Radio – football was Soccer (always with a capital S), and Soccer was 'grand'. Indeed most things in Charlie's world were grand. The players were grand, the matches were grand, the footballing life itself was grand.

Buchan's magazine first appeared in September 1951 (when Charlie was already aged 61), just as the Festival of Britain was winding down on London's South Bank. Rationing was still in place. Paper was still in short supply. National Service was still obligatory for young men, while thousands of British troops were serving in Korea.

In the six years since Hitler's defeat, attendance levels at English football had soared to record levels, topping 41 million in 1948–49. Yet never before had the fortunes of the national team been so low, following England's humiliating defeat by the USA during the 1950 World Cup in Brazil (a match witnessed by Buchan and several of the Fleet Street veterans who would become his regular contributors).

Thus hope for the future, in the bright new world of post-war Britain, was necessarily tempered by anxiety concerning the health of the national game. Similarly, parochial pride in our footballing greats had always to be counterbalanced by reluctant admiration for the obvious skills of those 'Continentals' and 'Latins' from overseas. Hot-headed and devious they may have been, but clearly they had much to teach us, about tactics, training, even what kind of boots to wear.

So successful was *Charles Buchan's Football Monthly* that in July 1953 the publishers issued the first *Charles Buchan's Soccer Gift Book*. For the next two decades this jaunty annual earned an automatic slot on the Christmas wish lists of thousands of schoolboys.

Buchan himself, despite his reporting commitments with the BBC and the *News Chronicle* – whose staff he had joined in 1928 after retiring from Arsenal – remained actively involved in both publications until his death in June 1960, while on holiday in Monte Carlo. He was a tall man, always immaculately dressed and unfailingly polite. Columnist John Macadam, another writer of the old school, said of him, 'Charles sees only the good in all men.' But whereas Macadam and several of his fellow writers were hard drinking adventurers, Buchan retained the image of a schoolmasterly gent. And yet in his prime he had been both a supremely gifted and wily inside forward – his ratio of 224 goals in 413 games for Sunderland still stands as a record – and a brave soldier, winning a Military Cross during the First World War (a fact he modestly omitted from his autobiography, published in 1955).

By 1958 *Football Monthly's* circulation had risen to 107,000, at which point the offices moved from the Strand to 161-166 Fleet Street.

By a curious coincidence, this was the site of Andertons Hotel, where the Football League had formed in 1888. Not only that but the new building, Hulton House, was owned by the former publishers of *Athletic News*, once Britain's most popular football weekly.

After Charlie's death the proprietors kept his name on the masthead (until 1971), and under new editor Pat Collins – buoyed up by England's World Cup victory in 1966 – increased circulation to 200,000 in 1968. The following year it reached an all-time peak of 254,000. Membership of the Boys' Club topped 100,000.

Changing fashions may explain part of the magazine's demise in the early 1970s. As hairstyles lengthened and trousers grew more flared, more young readers were veering away from programme and autograph swaps in favour of records and pop-related memorabilia. Football itself was entering a period of decline, as the ravages of hooliganism began to take their toll on attendances. Charlie's seemingly more innocent world was fading rapidly.

But also crucial was the decision by *Football Monthly's* new holding company, Longacre Press, to publish a sister magazine called *Goal*, in 1968. It took two years for *Goal* to outsell *Football Monthly*. Then a third contender materialised in the form of *Shoot*, a brash new weekly, published by IPC.

Shoot and *Goal* each sold over 220,000 copies weekly in 1971, compared with 164,000, and falling, for *Football Monthly*.

In August 1973 the publishers responded by rebranding the title in a smaller format. But as editor Pat Collins suspected, it was a losing battle, and in August 1974 the title left Fleet Street and became *Football Magazine*.

A golden era had truly passed.

The compilation which follows is selected from issues of *Charles Buchan's Football Monthly* dating 1951–73, and from the *Charles Buchan's Soccer Gift Books*, published annually from 1953–74.

Inevitably readers will spot gaps; star players unmentioned, key events uncovered. Some of these omissions arise from lack of space. Others are simply owing to the fact that the magazine and gift books were by no means comprehensive in their coverage. If there is a narrative in what follows, therefore, it is fractured rather than cohesive, though hopefully no less appealing when viewed as a whole.

It will be noted that this book forms part of *Played in Britain*, a series which seeks to celebrate and preserve these islands' extraordinary sporting heritage.

Heritage is generally thought to reside in historic buildings, in places and landscapes. What it is hoped the following pages demonstrate is that there is heritage in ephemera too, and in the shared narrative that make us a nation, and a footballing nation at that.

For more on the Charles Buchan archive, see our list of related publications on the back page.

RONNIE YEATS
(Liverpool)

Liverpool 1951-73

by Stephen Done
Curator of the Liverpool Football Club Museum at Anfield

When the first edition of *Charles Buchan's Football Monthly* hit the bookstands in September 1951, Liverpool Football Club appeared to be settling into a long and, some feared at the time, an irreversible period of decline and mediocrity.

Yet by the time the magazine bowed out in 1974, the Reds were not only established as one of the most feared outfits in the First Division, but were also set fair to become the dominant force in European football.

That this remarkable transition occurred almost exactly within the 23 year life span of *Charles Buchan's Football Monthly* was of course entirely coincidental.

Nor can it be claimed the following collection of articles and images conveys the full story of those extraordinary years. As a London-based publication *Football Monthly* did not always spread its favours evenly, and nor did it ever set out to be a journal of record.

Nevertheless, within this selection readers will find tantalising glimpses and snapshots of an era that laid the foundations for the club as we know it today.

As far as Liverpool are concerned, the Charles Buchan archive falls into two distinct periods: from 1951–59 (before the arrival of Bill Shankly), and from 1959–74 (the Shankly period itself).

But it would be quite wrong to suggest that Liverpool were bereft of all hope before Shankly.

Far from it. For Reds fans during the immediate post war period there seemed plenty of cause for optimism.

Despite its proximity to the docks in Bootle, Anfield had emerged miraculously unscathed from the attentions of the Luftwaffe, while the club lost only one player during hostilities. Tom Cooper, a classy right-back and former club captain, had been killed whilst riding a despatch motorbike in the blackout. (After his death, helmets were made compulsory by the Forces.)

Not all clubs suffered so lightly, and so overall the omens seemed positive as the Red Devils (as the team were briefly nicknamed at this time) – wearing mis-matched, faded and heavily darned kit in keeping with the austerity of the times – buckled down to win the League in the first full season after the war. This they achieved by pipping Manchester United by one point in June 1947, the season having been much delayed by a severe winter.

Not only was this the club's first title since 1923, but for a brief period the Double was on the cards, until, that is, Burnley halted Liverpool's progress in a replayed FA Cup semi-final.

But instead of manager George Kay building on this wonderful season – enjoyed by a record Anfield average gate of over 45,000 (far in excess of the pre-war norm) – the momentum was lost and it was left to other clubs, the likes of Wolves and Portsmouth, to dominate the ensuing boom years.

Not least among the ascendant powers were those other Red Devils, of Old Trafford, managed by the former Liverpool player Matt Busby. (Busby, incidentally, had been offered the role of coach at Anfield in 1945. How different the course of post war footballing history might have been had he accepted it.)

Further disappointment for Liverpool followed on a drearily wet day at Wembley in April 1950.

Expecting to beat Arsenal and bring the elusive FA Cup to Anfield for the first time, instead George Kay's team succumbed 2-0. Kay, his health now failing after 14 years in the job, had to shoulder much of the criticism, having dropped the very player who had scored Liverpool's winner in the semi-final, against Everton.

Thus Bob Paisley was denied his tilt at Wembley glory, while Kay was replaced in March 1951, somewhat surprisingly, by Don Welsh, a former Charlton player whose natural ebullience seemingly outweighed (at least to the Liverpool board) his lack of success during four previous years in the hotseat at Third Division Brighton.

As *Football Monthly* made its debut therefore, Liverpool appeared to be entering a new era under Welsh, even if, as results would soon show, the rot was by then too deep to cure. (As for Paisley, the great Liverpool stalwart retired from playing three years later and thereby remained almost entirely absent from the pages of *Football Monthly*, leaving it to later magazines such as *Shoot* and *Goal* to record his emergence between 1974–83 as the most successful manager of the 20th century.)

But if, in *Football Monthly*'s early years, Liverpool as a club were hardly centre stage, there was one Anfield regular whom Charles Buchan clearly admired.

Featured on the cover of the November 1952 edition (*see page 13*), winger Billy Liddell was the embodiment of every quality Buchan looked for in a professional.

Born in Dunfermline, Liddell had signed for Liverpool from Lochgelly Violet in July 1938, and, in common with Bob Paisley, had been about to break into the first team when war intervened the following year. Immediately Liddell signed up for the RAF, and although he played as a guest for a variety of clubs in war-time competitions, it was seven years before he made his League debut for Liverpool, in September 1946.

Understandably throughout the early years of *Football Monthly*, tales of the privations and the camaraderie of war featured frequently. Buchan himself had served heroically in the trenches during 1914–18, while for readers, the Second World War, and subsequently the experience of national service (until it ended in 1960), created a real bond between themselves and the players. Even if few footballing heroes had become war heroes, the majority had endured their share of square bashing. And they all enjoyed jokes about the sergeant major.

For Liddell however, the consquences of war can best be summed up by statistics.

'The neat destroyer,' as co-editor John Thompson described him in 1952, scored 228 goals in 534 appearances for Liverpool between 1946–61. Yet had he not been denied those seven 'missing' seasons from 1939–46, Liddell would easily have outdone both Roger Hunt (245 goals) and Ian Rush (229) to become Liverpool's leading scorer of all time.

And as Hunt himself later commented, Liddell achieved all that he did on the pitch despite training only two mornings a week while continuing to work as an accountant in the city centre.

Small wonder that Liddell the player and Liddell the man drew praise in equal measure. As Buchan wrote in August 1959, after Liddell had been crowned as *Football Monthly*'s Footballer of the Year, 'Not only is he one of the greatest forwards in the soccer world, but he is a qualified accountant, a Justice of the Peace and, in his spare time, a big coaching help to soccer-minded youths.'

Buchan could have added that Liddell was a Sunday School teacher, neither smoked nor drank, was a tireless worker for charity and local boys clubs, and a pioneer of hospital radio. ▶

◀ 1963–64 Gift Book

Above all, *Football Monthly* lauded Liddell's loyalty. A player of his stature, it was said, could easily have agitated for a move to a superior club, yet he stayed loyal to Liverpool, or 'Liddellpool' as they were sometimes called, even as the Reds stumbled their way towards relegation to the Second Division in 1954 (ironically to be replaced by newly promoted Everton).

Liddell apart, only a few Liverpool players appeared in *Football Monthly* during the mid 1950s. One was Jimmy Payne, the 'Merseyside Matthews' who notched up 43 goals in 243 games before being surprisingly sold to Everton for £5,000 in 1956. Perhaps Don Welsh was prescient, because Payne managed only a handful of games across Stanley Park before being forced to retire from injury.

Also featured was Alan A'Court, who despite his romantic name came from Rainhill and had been signed as a youth from Prescot Cables. In the August 1956 edition A'Court partly ascribed Liverpool's relegation form two years previously to a pre-season tour to the USA and Canada (a repeat of a tour previously undertaken in 1946, when Liverpool's war-weary players apparently feasted on unrationed meat). Even in 1953, suggested A'Court, the excitement of being given a 'daily dollar allowance' and being 'allowed to go and buy meals whenever we liked' had taken its toll. Rationing, it should be added, ended in Britain only in July 1954.

But the problems facing Liverpool clearly ran deeper than nutrition.

After two seasons in Division Two, and despite finishing in third place in 1956, with an ageing team and little money for new signings, Don Welsh was sacked.

In his place the board promoted Phil Taylor, a former player who had joined the coaching staff two years earlier. In later years such

appointments from within became known as the 'Liverpool Way'. But in 1956 the choice may well have been influenced by the club's bank manager more than by footballing considerations.

One of the more enigmatic characters in Liverpool's managerial history, Bristol-born Taylor, who once played county cricket for Gloucestershire, had been signed for £5,000 in 1936 as an 18 year old prodigy. Holding the backline with Matt Busby, he soon gained a reputation as a class player, earning three caps for England. The war saw him guarding railway viaducts along the west coast mainline, after which he played a key role in the 1946-47 League Championship side. He also captained the losing team in the 1950 FA Cup final.

Under Taylor Liverpool fought gamely to regain their First Division status, finishing third in both 1956 and 1957.

Yet for all his gentlemanly qualities – attributes that Buchan so admired – Taylor barely featured in *Football Monthly* during his three years at the Anfield helm.

But then Second Division status meant that several key players from this era have also remained largely forgotten. For example Essex-born Johnny Evans, who described the Kop as 'a crowd of open mouths and roaring voices' and was the first Liverpool player to score five goals in a game since Andy McGuigan in 1902, went on to notch up an impressive 53 goals in 107 games.

Handsome and entertaining, in different circumstances Evans might have been a star. Yet he was sold to Colchester in November 1957.

Four months later, just after the Munich Air Disaster, in what was by then a rare Liverpool feature (*see pages 24-25*), *Football Monthly*'s cameras captured in colour five other players in the Anfield dressing room during this time of transition.

With hindsight, the choice of players appears apt, capturing as it did a glimpse of a squad that was about to experience a seismic shift

Jimmy Melia, pictured bizarrely wearing a shirt and tie whilst on the physio's table, hailed from the 'Scottie Road', and with nearly 80 goals in 286 games would survive the great Anfield shake up, as did Alan A'Court and Warrington-born full back John Molyneux.

Molyneux, it should be noted, was photographed holding the latest in training footwear, a 'Converse All Stars' baseball boot.

Veteran right half John Wheeler was another popular local, taking over from Liddell as captain and being an ever-present during the following season. Wheeler made history by scoring a hat-trick in four minutes against Port Vale in November 1956.

Welshman Antonio 'Tony' Rowley also made his name with a hat-trick, on his debut in 1953. But in common with that other prolific scorer, Johnny Evans, Rowley's 39 goals in 63 games were still not enough, and by the time his portait appeared in the magazine he had been sold to Tranmere. (Curiously, his tenure as the Reds' inside-right briefly coincided with the appearance of one Anthony Arthur Rowley, no relation, at inside left.)

As players came and went, Liverpool's media profile remained almost as static as did their League position. A fourth place finish in 1958 was repeated the following season, leading finally to Taylor's resignation in November 1959.

Nobody showed more heartfelt regret than Taylor himself. 'I made (promotion) my goal,' he told the *Liverpool Echo*. 'I set my heart on it and strove for it with all the energy I could muster. Such striving has not been enough and now the time has come to hand over to someone else to see if they can do better.'

Though still aged only 42, Taylor never managed again.

The person to whom the board now turned was of course the feisty Scot, Bill Shankly. Then aged 46, Shankley had previously managed Carlisle, Grimsby, Workington and most recently Second Division promotion-hopefuls, Huddersfield.

Having served his apprenticeship at clubs with lesser potential, Shankly's arrival in December 1959 was a moment of profound significance in the history of Liverpool. As every club history has recorded, Shankly and his cohorts in the bootroom (Bob Paisley, Reuben Bennett, Joe Fagan and later Ronnie Moran) created the Anfield ethos on which the very foundation of the club is built today.

Yet at the time, Shankly's appointment, at a salary of £2,500 per annum, caused barely a stir outside Merseyside, and for his first few seasons in the job, for all his later reputation as a fast-talking, hard-hitting man of the people, he maintained a relatively low profile – as reflected by only occasional mentions in *Football Monthly*.

In his first two seasons Shankly did no better than to emulate Phil Taylor, finishing third on both occasions.

Only in his third season, after signing two young Scots, Ron Yeats and Ian St John – to add to Gordon Milne (*opposite, left*), signed from his old club Preston – did Shankly achieve the long awaited breakthrough.

With youngsters Peter Thompson, Ian Callaghan and Roger Hunt settling into the team, Liverpool ran away with the Second Division title in 1962.

Behind the scenes, meanwhile, Shankly was learning fast that the biggest obstacle to success at Anfield was the reluctance of the stuffed shirts in the boardroom to relinquish their control of team

▲ May 1965

▲ April 1965

affairs. Phil Taylor had been too gentlemanly to resist, and it had cost him his job. Shankly, anxious to relaunch the club 'like a rocket to the moon,' was less circumspect.

Yet just as the Reds were preparing for their first season in the top flight for eight years, that August the Anfield board decided to sell gifted winger Johnny Morrissey – to Everton of all clubs – without consulting the manager.

Shankly was incandescent and had actually cleared his desk before being persuaded to return to the club office and settle the matter. This he did by delivering chairman Tom Williams a fiercely worded ultimatum. Either the board hand over to him full control over team selection, all player dealings and scouting, and at the same time pledge to invest more on transfers and on the modernisation of Anfield and the training ground at Melwood, or he really would resign.

The old days of amateur directors ruling the roost were over. This was now the 1960s. It was time for professionalism at *all* levels.

Shankly's bullying of the board finally worked. But equally, his renewed determination galvanised both his players and the supporters. Only after this watershed did the Shankly legend start to build.

Even then, most of his efforts were directed to the job at hand and not to the media. Thus as the spotlight fell increasingly on Liverpool from 1962 onwards – League champions in 1964 and 1966, FA Cup winners (at last!) in 1965, European Cup Winners Cup finalists in 1966 – it was not until April 1966 that *Football Monthly* published a feature specifically on Shankly the man.

Such circumspection concerning a charismatic top-flight manager would be unthinkable in today's press. But then, compared with today's reporting, the press of that

era barely reported anything beyond team matters. None of the crucial changes in the Anfield boardroom were ever alluded to – for example the greater involvement of the Moores family (of Littlewoods fame) – and only once during the entire 1960s did *Football Monthly* even mention the name of Tom Williams' successor as club chairman, Sidney Reakes, and that was only in passing.

Instead, the players were the stars. Just take the team group featured in July 1965 – still, it will be noted, wearing the white shorts that would be jettisoned in favour of an all-red kit the following season.

These were the men who established Liverpool's dominance of the period: Lawrence, Byrne, Lawler, Milne, Yeats, Stevenson, Callaghan, Hunt, St John, Smith and Thompson.

To Reds fans of the era their very names read like a poem, and every one of them was either signed by Shankly or plucked by him from the junior or reserve teams.

Willie Stevenson, making little headway at Rangers, had been contemplating emigration to Australia before Shankly signed him from Ibrox. Fellow Scotsman Tommy Lawrence (*above right*), the 'Flying Pig', had spent five years at Anfield before stepping up to the first team in 1963. Gerry Byrne, later billed by Shankly as 'the hardest player I've ever seen,' had been stuck in the reserves and was actually on the transfer list when Shankly recognised his potential.

And while the rest of Liverpool, the Kop included, was swaying to the sounds of the newly emerging Merseybeat and letting their hair down in Beatles' mop-tops, Shankly and his bootroom team steadily built an ethos rooted in hard work, professionalism and a ruthless desire to win. No slackers, no wide boys, no fancy dans.

As we can discern from the interview with Ron Yeats in October 1962, Liverpool's promotion squad of that year was made up of perhaps the last generation of players to have shared lifestyles similar to those of the managers and coaches of the post war era.

After leaving school 'Rowdy' Yeats had served his apprenticeship as a slaughterman in Aberdeen, starting work at four o'clock in the morning. He then made his Scottish League debut with Dundee United, before being called up to the Army and posted to Aldershot. By the time Bill Shankly came calling for his signature at an Edinburgh Hotel in 1961, Yeats was exhausted by all the travel, to and fro, between army camps and football grounds at opposite ends of the country.

But Shankly, like Matt Busby and many others, had been there before him, during the war years, and as a fellow Scot and, in Yeats' words, as 'a great talker' he soon convinced the young centre half that Anfield was the place. 'You'll be going to a club booked for promotion,' enthused Shanks. And so it proved.

At times during the mid 1960s it seemed as if the city of Liverpool, for all its crumbling infrastructure and economic woes, was the very centre of the universe.

In the midst of crippling urban decline, the city's working class poets, its pop stars, comedians and footballers, all somehow reached a crescendo together.

Now the Reds became regulars on the pages of *Football Monthly*. The Kop, heralded for its collective wit and rendition of popular favourites, gained frequent mentions too, famously singing 'Ee-aye-addio, Harold's still in bed,' outside Number 10 Downing Street after beating Leeds in the 1965 FA Cup Final. (Prime Minister Harold Wilson was MP for the Merseyside constituency of Huyton.)

Ian St John told the magazine, 'There's no noise like the Anfield noise - and I like it!' The Anfield crowd, 'are terrific, compelling you always to go all out.'

Staff writer (and later editor) Pat Collins, a Londoner, was similarly awe-struck in a report in 1966. 'Nowhere are there fans to match their spontaneity, their wit or the sharp edge of their sarcasm in song. Nobody is spared or overlooked. No name or situation stumps them.'

The mainstream media caught on too. BBC TV's *Panorama* exalted the Kop as Liverpool's latest cultural contribution to the Swinging Sixties. BBC Radio's normally staid *Desert Island Discs* programme had Bill Shankly as its guest on Cup Final day, 1965. The players listened to the programme on the team coach's radio as they drove to Wembley.

Even the football correspondent of *The Times*, Geoffrey Green, could scarcely contain himself.

'Merseyside does not care to live on the side of mercy,' he waxed in the April 1963 edition of *Football Monthly*. 'The tides of enthusiasm that sweep the city of Liverpool are far too strong... Perhaps it is the salt in the nearby sea in their veins... whatever it is, the feeling hits you like the blast of a furnace, like the sharp threat of a sword drawn from its scabbard.'

Green contended that in Liverpool there was no half-way house. You were either Red or Blue. Comedian Ken Dodd agreed. He was a Red through and through, he revealed in the 1965–66 *Gift Book*. And in order to keep up with football, he joked, he bought *Charles Buchan's Football Monthly* every week!

But whilst the photo of Dodd training at Anfield is a classic, the magazine missed out on an even more bizarre exposition of the synthesis between football and show business; a 'photo op' in which Dodd, Billy Liddell, Ian St ▶

John and Ron Yeats, complete with Beatles wigs, mimed on stage to the latest Fab Four single.

By 1968 *Football Monthly*'s offices were on the same floor in Fleet Street as *Disc*, so stars were often to be seen in the corridors. Added to this, the publishers were not shy of straying into the world of pop. In 1963 they produced a supplement on Billy Fury, better known in the Dingle area of Liverpool as Ronnie Wycherley.

Then along came Cilla Black. One half of her family was Red, the other Blue, she trilled, but now she was a Red because that was her fiancé's allegiance.

Yet if this sounds as if Liverpool Football Club were caught up in a brave new world of 1960s froth, the reality was anything but.

The club itself did virtually nothing to exploit the city's rising fame. Other than hire a disc jockey to play the latest hits on Anfield's new public address system – *You'll Never Walk Alone* by Gerry and the Pacemakers most notably – it was left to the Kop to form the bridge between football and pop culture.

Nor were there any George Best figures at Anfield. As Shankly made clear, celebrity had to be earned on the pitch, not in boutiques or nightclubs.

The Kop idols were instead Ian St John, a no-nonsense hard grafting Scot, and their very own knight, 'Sir Roger' Hunt, an unassuming and distinctly untrendy goal machine.

Nothing characterised this apparent lack of gloss at Anfield better than the home-made replica of a trophy first seen in the June 1964 edition.

In only their second season back at the top, Liverpool had just beaten Arsenal 5-0 to win their first League title since 1947.

But the previous holders of the Championship, Everton, had refused to hand over the trophy for the final Saturday, forcing Liverpool to improvise. This they did, courtesy of two fans, Terry and Teddy Curlett who, in best *Blue Peter* tradition, used a combination of plastic, cardboard, glue and paint to fashion a substitute on their kitchen table.

There it is on page 42, being held aloft by Ron Yeats, as Bill Shankly (helpfully arrowed by the magazine) waves to the Anfield crowd on this day of jubilation.

Two years later it made a second appearance in the last frame of the Roger Hunt Star Strip (*page 46*), showing the Reds perform their lap of honour after winning the League title again in 1966.

We get a third glimpse of the plastic trophy on the dressing room table on page 69.

It was almost as if this simple piece of folk-art was held in higher esteem by Shankly than the real silverware. Which, in a sense it still is, for it is now on permanent display in the club museum.

Still on the theme of trophies, for most football fans the year 1966 conjures up memories of the World Cup. But for fans on Merseyside there arguably came an even more precious moment, as captured in the October 1966 edition.

True, England had won the World Cup, thanks to contributions from players on both sides of Stanley Park, but only months earlier Liverpool had won the League and Everton the FA Cup. This meant that in August 1966 members of both teams were able to parade all three trophies – the real ones this time – around Goodison Park, as the two teams prepared to contest a fourth, the Charity Shield.

Never before or since have any city football rivals paraded so much valuable silverware in one place at one time.

But as the record books show, the Reds were merely warming up. As the 1970s began Liverpool stepped up a further gear to become even more relentless in their pursuit of honours.

'Sir Roger' moved on. Tony Hateley moved in, only to be quickly superceded by football's first £100,000 teenager, Alun Evans, a rare pin up on the Anfield scene and one who was unlucky not to prosper.

In Emlyn Hughes, signed from Blackpool, Anfield found another rock, one whose infectious enthusiasm made him an instant hit. 'To lose is a sin - to be avoided at all costs,' he said after sampling the Liverpool training methods.

In article after article the same phrases appeared. Will to win. Passion. Never-say-die.

Of Tommy Smith, made captain by Shankly in 1970 despite their often difficult relationship, the manager said, 'There is no one in the game doing the job he has been doing for Liverpool. It will be nothing but an injustice from the game itself if he hangs up his boots without having won at least one international honour.'

Always playing mind games, Shankly persuaded his own men that they were indeed the best, and that the opposition were just lambs for the slaughter.

And yet his final crop of newcomers, among them John Toshack from Swansea in 1970 and Kevin Keegan from Scunthorpe in 1971 (signed in a deal Shankly admitted was 'daylight robbery'), were a world apart from their predecessors of the 1950s and 1960s, and not only in terms of their hairstyles.

Two of them, Steve Heighway and Brian Hall, were even university graduates, dubbed 'Big Bamber' and 'Little Bamber' respectively (after Bamber Gascoigne, the *University Challenge* quizmaster). It was Heighway who coined the phrase, 'the Liverpool Way', to encapsulate the almost institutional rigour which encouraged players such as himself to make a smooth transition from the dressing room to the bootroom, and in a few cases, from the bootroom to the manager's office.

In the June 1972 issue of *Football Monthly,* Stan Liversedge correctly predicted that Liverpool were to be the 'Team of the Seventies'. The following season witnessed not only another Championship victory, but Shankly finally secured Liverpool's first European trophy, the UEFA Cup. Shankly was then to lead Liverpool to a further FA Cup win, in a total demolition of in-form Newcastle United, in 1974.

But then, again purely by coincidence, events took a quite unexpected turn.

Undone by its brasher weekly counterparts, *Football Monthly* finally folded in mid 1974, while at almost exactly the same time, citing that he had 'conquered Everest' with the club, in July 1974 the great Shankly asked that his contract not be renewed.

Anfield was stunned. The entire football world was stunned. Bob Paisley, his unwilling successor, was more stunned than anyone. Shankly was not yet 61. Surely he was leaving the game too soon.

Accordingly, our selection ends with an image from the last ever *Charles Buchan Gift Book,* published that summer. There stands a coiffured Kevin Keegan in his flares and heels, facing a young boy of the same name, on the stairs leading down to the pitch. Over the door to the players' tunnel hangs the sign, 'This is Anfield.'

One of the most potent symbols of English football, the sign had been placed there by Shankly during the 1960s, to put the fear of God into opposition players.

On the whole, it had worked.

CHARLES BUCHAN'S FOOTBALL MONTHLY

1/6

NOVEMBER 1952

Inside:

MY STORY by JIMMY DICKINSON

Full-page Pictures

KEN PLANT
TOM FINNEY
JACK BADHAM
LESLIE BENNETT
DOUG LISHMAN
JIM TODD
ALF BELLIS

Edited by
CHARLES BUCHAN
and
JOHN THOMPSON

BILLY LIDDELL
(Liverpool and Scotland)

BILLY LIDDELL, THE NEAT "DESTROYER"

THERE is a neat and compact Scottish look about Billy Liddell. His features are vaguely reminiscent of his fellow-countryman, Benny Lynch. And into his shooting boots Liddell packs the power and the perfect timing which the mighty little champion held in his clenched fists.

Lynch punched as though it cost him no effort at all. That is the way Liddell kicks. His foot is drawn back less than most men's, the follow-through is brief and unspectacular. Yet the ball seems to explode off his foot—straight and true and terribly strong.

In an age in which wing-forwards rarely slam the ball into the back of the net, rarely cut directly for goal, the Liverpool and Scotland outside-left stands almost alone. He smacks the ball as Jimmy Dimmock did ; he sums-up a situation with the split-second reckoning which made Eric Brook so dangerous.

Other wingers may surpass Liddell in the subtleties, many have more frills. But none can better the manner in which he brings the ball under instant control and either hits it or, in indisputable possession, moves away.

He is as unpretentious off the field as he is on it and is the least flamboyant of stars.

Liddell seems to scorn superfluous decoration. His football has the look of a destroyer stripped for action. It has the same threat, the same deadliness.

Yet this great footballer, this man who is more of a potential match-winner than any other winger in the world, has never figured in the transfer market. He cost Liverpool only his £10 signing-on fee.

A Liddell in the red jersey of Liverpool seems to be a fixture. I cannot remember even a rumour that he might leave Anfield. Not for the quiet Scot the publicity which discontent brings, not for him the restlessness which provokes huge bids and irritating " will he, won't he," controversy in the newspapers.

Liddell joined Liverpool after careful consideration. He judged wisely and has no regrets.

Looking back on his life it is not difficult to visualise how he gained his mastery in kicking and controlling the ball with both feet. His adaptability doubtless stems from his schooldays.

He was a sturdy little centre-half before he led the Dunfermline Schoolboys' attack. Against Ireland he was the Scottish boys' outside-right. He even had a crack at Rugby.

Then, as a junior, he played so well for Lochgelly Violet that a message about his talent to George Kay sent the Liverpool manager rushing north.

But before Liddell moved to Merseyside the level-headed youth, wisely guided by his parents, made many inquiries about his future—with particular reference to his prospects for continuing his accountancy studies.

He graduated to the football heights the only way there is—with game after game in mid-week soccer, with the third team, with hours of patient practice and careful listening to older players, sifting and selecting their hints, adapting them to his own temperament and style.

PROFILE
by
JOHN THOMPSON

Gradually his play took shape. His power increased. In the spring of 1940 he was a first team player. Soon representative team selectors noticed him.

The Scots took the exile to their hearts. Billy Liddell's stature was such that it overcame even Glasgow's queer prejudice against " Anglos."

He played in all three Victory games and won his first real caps against Wales and Ireland in the season of 1946-47.

His highest honour was selection for the Great Britain side against the Rest of Europe in 1947, and it is a reflection of his consistency that, five years later, most of us would plump for Liddell at outside-left if another British side had to be chosen.

He has told me that his first soccer memory is of seeing Alan Morton playing for Rangers against Cowdenbeath when he was ten.

" I always enjoyed games," he said, " Running errands I would dribble tennis balls along the pavement."

Of his first international Liddell said : " At half-time I wondered what had hit me I was so excited. I had to have two aspirins to clear my head. . ."

Ask him to name the best full-backs he has met and he will reply : " That's difficult to say—probably Carey, Shimwell and Woodruffe. All have keen anticipation, positional sense and ability to tackle quickly."

To young players his advice is : " Keep a level head. Practice hard and often—and make sure you have another trade at your finger-tips. The player without worries is the successful player."

He helped Liverpool reach the F.A. Cup Final, only to suffer the disappointment of defeat by Arsenal. He scored a brilliant hat-trick last season against the polished marking of Tottenham's Alf Ramsey.

Perhaps of far more importance than all Liddell's achievements was the example he was setting to the soccer-crazy kids of Merseyside, an example of modesty and concentration, team-spirit and sportsmanship.

Many players receive the hero-worship of their young followers. Billy Liddell more than most of our sporting idols, deserves it.

▲ November 1952

SPOTLIGHT ON LIVERPOOL

THOUGH Liverpool have been one of the most consistent teams in the country, with an unbroken stay in the First Division since 1905, they have never won the F.A. Cup.

Twice they have got into the Final. The first time, in 1914, they were beaten at the Crystal Palace by Burnley, with a goal scored by centre-forward Bert Freeman.

This was the first occasion a Final tie was watched by the reigning monarch : H.M. King George V. It was the last final at the Palace.

Then in 1950, Arsenal beat them at Wembley by two goals from inside-left Reg Lewis. It was the season Liverpool had set up a First Division record by playing through the opening 19 League games without defeat.

Twice finalists, six times semi-finalists. That is Liverpool's record in the Cup. You can never write them off in this competition. They are capable of pulling out a classic display on the big occasion.

Unhappily for them, they have been handicapped by injuries this season. When they promised big things at the start, misfortune overtook them in the absence, through injuries, of star players.

Nevertheless, they are still in a prominent position in the League table. With great players like full-back Lambert, half-backs Jones and Hughes, and wing forwards Payne and Liddell, they can still challenge for the championship which they last won in 1947, by a point from Manchester United and Wolves.

It is strange, though, that there is only one Scot in the present team, Billy Liddell, Scottish international outside-left. Scots played a big part in putting Liverpool on the Soccer map.

At first, the team was all Scotsmen. They won the Lancashire League and Liverpool Cup in their opening season.

It must have been galling to the men from across the border when the Liverpool Cup presented to them was stolen.

Liverpool F.C. : Back row—Jones, Spicer, Lambert, Ashcroft, Heydon, Hughes, Mr. D. Welsh (manager).
Front row—Baron, Paisley, Liddell, Taylor, Payne, Smith, Brierley.

▲ February 1953

It cost the club something like £130 to replace the trophy. A lot of money way back in 1892 !

Among the great Scots who have worn the famous colours were goalkeepers Ted Doig and Kenny Campbell, full-back Billy Dunlop, with the snow-white hair, big, blond centre-half Alex Raisbeck, and sturdy Donald McKinley.

They will never be forgotten.

Nor will the former secretary, Tom Watson, pass easily from mind. Tom could never watch his team play. Usually he paced up and down behind the grand-stand, listening to the roars of the crowd.

Really, it was a quarrel over rent that brought Liverpool into being as a first-class club.

In 1892, Everton played at Anfield Road, but when it was proposed to increase the rent, many of their officials protested, walked out of the place and established themselves at Goodison Park.

A few officials remained at Anfield.

With the landlord, Mr. John Houlding, who became the first president, they founded the present Liverpool.

The new club had a sensational start. In the first five seasons they won the Lancashire Combination and Liverpool Cup, secured admission to the Football League, won promotion to the First Division, were relegated a season later, and, the following year, won their way back to the top circle.

It was without parallel in League history and stamped Liverpool as one of the great teams of the future.

During this time, they set up one record that, in these days when competition is so greatly increased in intensity, is unlikely to be equalled.

In 1893-4, they went through the 28 Second Division games without defeat, winning 22 and drawing six. Of course, they ran away with the championship, eight points ahead of Small Heath.

There is another proud feather in the Liverpool cap. In 1904-05, they won the Second Division championship.

Twelve months later, they carried off the First Division title with a clear margin of four points over Preston North End.

Only Everton, in 1931 and 1932, and Tottenham Hotspur, in 1950 and 1951, have also won the championships of the Second and First Divisions in successive seasons.

Ever since their wonderful start, Liverpool have been blessed with great goalkeepers—as Everton have been noted for their half-backs, and Tranmere Rovers for their centre-forwards.

Ray Lambert, one of Liverpool's great players, who will help to keep the club in the limelight this season.

Doig and Campbell have already been mentioned, but there were also Willie and Elisha Scott, Sam Hardy, generally recognised as the "prince of goalkeepers," and the South African Arthur Riley.

Elisha Scott holds the record number of thirty-one appearances for his native country, Ireland.

There is a story on Merseyside that once, when Scott was walking down a Liverpool street, he met Dixie Dean, Everton's great centre-forward, renowned for the number of goals he scored with his head.

As they approached, Dean nodded. Scott immediately dived full length !

Now Liverpool have Charlie Ashcroft. He has already played in F.A. representative games and for England "B" teams. He will soon join the list of Liverpool's international goalkeepers.

It was in 1924 that Liverpool set the fashion by introducing South Africans to League football.

In that year the South Africans sent a touring team to this country.

There was a great stir when Liverpool persuaded three of them to stay behind. One was Riley, another Gordon Hodgson, a splendid six-footer who could take any of the inside-forward positions with distinction. He played several times for England.

Then, in 1933, Liverpool got Berry

Nieuwenhuys—better known as Nivvy—a tall, slender outside-right with twinkling feet.

Liverpool have a soft spot for South Africans, who have served them well and brought honour to the club.

Though the F.A. Cup has eluded them, Liverpool have been League champions five times.

Their greatest era came between 1921 and 1923, when they won the First Division title two years in succession.

They were a grand, solid and clever combination, with a half-back line—McNab, Wadsworth, McKinley—that has seldom been surpassed in effectiveness.

With inside forward Harry Chambers and Dick Forshaw to round off the movements, Liverpool were undoubtedly the best team in the land during that spell.

There have been other great Liverpool teams, and hard-working managers, like George Kay and the present Don Welsh, who have kept the club among the top-notchers.

And famous men like the late John McKenna, Football League president, have set a standard of sportsmanship that has always flown high.

Liverpool have carried the Soccer banner all over the globe—Europe, South Africa, Canada, America. They have been a credit to the game wherever they have been.

IT was a May morning in 1950. Within a few hours I was to play for Liverpool in the Cup Final. Oh, what a wonderful morning! Little did I realise that very soon it would look more wonderful—but that the day would not end on such a happy note.

Feeling happy, I bought a paper and turned to the sports pages to see what had been written about the big game:

First thing I noted was the England selection for the close-season tour. Our left-half, Bill Jones, was named. "How excited he will be," I thought.

I read down the list. "Payne, Liverpool. Payne . . . that's me, I'm on the 'B' tour," I gasped.

You can imagine my excitement. After only a couple of years as a first team player, and on the very day I was to play in the Cup Final at Wembley—there came this honour.

"Surely this is a good omen for this afternoon's Final," I thought, as team-mates congratulated me.

Unfortunately it wasn't. Arsenal beat us 2—0, their scorer being Reg Lewis, who partnered me a few days later in my first international.

We had been confident of winning, but Arsenal were one up after 15 minutes and got another after the interval. Even then we were not finished, and I think Arsenal owe more to goal-keeper George Swindin than they will ever realise.

Liverpool flung everything into attack, determined to pull level, and Billy Liddell, breaking away, put across a peach of a centre. Swindin palmed the ball out and I flung myself forward to head.

"Goal! It's a goal!" The shout of triumph was in my throat—when the goalkeeper made an incredible save. How he got into position I will never know.

I don't think he knew himself. But the main thing was that he had stopped a goal which would have spurred us on to fight harder.

Soon after this Final I was off to Italy, Holland and Luxembourg. In spite of the disappointment at losing the Cup I was in good spirits. So were my "B" team-mates—but not for long.

Italy smashed us 5—0, at Milan. They were the finest team I had seen; they played fast, Continental style.

On to Holland we went and lost 3—0, in Amsterdam. My only highlight of this game was partnering Eddie Quigley. A fine player to have alongside one, he is a perfect passer of the ball. He clips it to within inches of any spot he desires.

So we moved to Luxembourg two games down, and with eight goals against us and none scored. It was our last match and we gained small consolation from a 2—1 win.

I might never have had these thrills had I not decided to switch to Liverpool, after going for a trial to Everton.

I went to the Goodison Park ground, but changed my mind and crossed over to the nearby Liverpool club.

Inside-forward or wing-half, I played in both positions until August, 1948. Then a regular winger was injured, I tried the position in practice, and was promoted to the senior team at the start of the season.

Bolton were our first opponents, and I did not do too badly. Then we met Arsenal—and my opponents were Bryn Jones, who had switched to wing-half, and Walley Barnes.

The mere mention of the names of such stars was enough to unsettle a youngster, but my third outing was even more an ordeal. We met Everton, at Goodison,

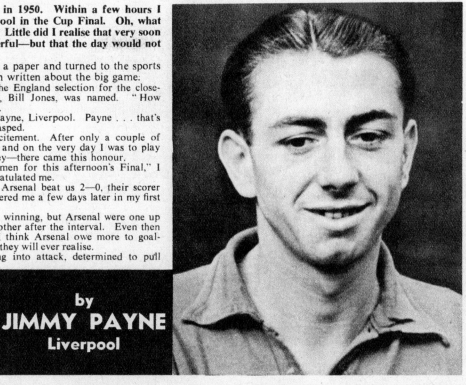

by
JIMMY PAYNE
Liverpool

Oh, what a wonderful morning...!

BUT UNFORTUNATELY, NOT A WONDERFUL DAY

before a record crowd of 79,000 flag-waving, rattle-whirring fans. "Derby" games are always tough, because of the partisan element, and these Liverpool-Everton games are as exciting as any Cup Final. The most dramatic tussle with our neighbours was in the 1950 semi-final. Excitement seethed in the town for weeks before the match, and anyone with a ticket to spare could get twenty times its value if he wished. We were plagued at home by callers and letter-writers, all of whom tried to prove a distant relationship plus a right to a ticket.

We got through by two clear goals, the second being scored by Billy Liddell, a player to whom I owe the majority of my scoring opportunities. This bustling Scot is my selection as the best match-winner of recent years. Fast, and with a tremendous shot, he wins games with opportunist goals which most players would not dream of attempting.

We struck up a wing-to-wing partnership which was of value to both of us. I tried to follow his example of hitting the ball right across the goal so that the other winger could run in and shoot or head.

After a time we also started inter-changing for a part of the game. This brought many match-winning moves.

Another player of great help in my early days was wing-half Phil Taylor. Always neat and trim in person, Phil's game was in the same pattern. He kept the ball on the ground and sent out a stream of passes.

He reminded me of my former idol, Matt Busby. Phil would have won a stack of honours, but for the intense competition for the England wing-half positions.

"Henry likes to listen to the football results, mother!"

ALAN A'COURT
Liverpool
asks
How would you like a trip to America with expenses paid?

A'Court "walked on air" when he heard he had been chosen.

IT HAPPENED TO ME WHEN I WAS ONLY EIGHTEEN

Can you imagine anything more wonderful for an eighteen-year-old than a two-month trip to America, with all expenses paid, pocket money provided, and wages? Sounds wonderful, doesn't it? Believe me, it was.

I was picked for Liverpool's close-season tour of the United States in 1953. In the previous season I had made my debut for Liverpool and had played a dozen games. I was by no means a regular, and so it did not occur to me that I might be in the tour party.

When we were told who were going I could hardly believe it when I heard that I was included. I walked on air for days !

Yet, as the season drew to a close, there were gloomy faces round Anfield, despite the tour.

(*Continued on page* 18)

Nothing doubtful about this goal banged in by A'Court (left) against Plymouth.

▲ August 1956

ALAN A'COURT

We were having a struggle to keep clear of the relegation area. In the final game of the season against Chelsea, we needed two points to stay up.

We got them . . . tension eased, and everyone was cheerful as we prepared for our wonderful journey.

We had five days on the Queen Mary, enjoying the ship's games, scoffing good food. Then, New York.

Liverpool had a good record in America and Canada from previous tours, and we wanted to maintain it.

Substitutes were allowed, and time and time again, I took over from an injured colleague.

The two final games were hectic. We turned out against the touring Irish international eleven, in Toronto, and won 3—1.

It was a very fine performance because they had a strong side, with players like Len Graham (Doncaster), Norman Uprichard (Portsmouth), Johnny Scott (Manchester United) and Eddie McMorran (Doncaster).

This game was played on a Saturday and, when it was over, we immediately caught a plane for New York, where we were due to play the Young Swiss side from Berne.

Our arrival time was around two o'clock in the morning and so a very tired eleven turned out in the afternoon. But we managed to hang on for a draw—the only game out of ten we failed to win.

I think the long tour may have had some effect on our play the following season for we were relegated. I know that I felt a bit jaded during the season.

But we also had some really wretched luck. The ball did not run at all kindly, numerous games were lost by an odd

" Wake up dear ! You must be dreaming about the Rovers—you keep groaning ! "

goal and we had a bad blow when full-back Eddie Spicer broke a leg.

Two highlights in my career, one a game against Everton in an F.A. Cup-tie, and one for the F.A. versus the R.A.F.

The local tussle with Everton was before a 72,000 crowd, at Goodison Park, and before kick-off, we were rated the underdogs.

Our 4—0 win staggered the crowd . . . even including our own fans who, nevertheless, were overjoyed at the success.

Our second goal came through a tip from a fan. He wrote to Don Welsh, who was then our manager, and told him that our opponents had a habit of moving up when a free kick was taken to play the opposing forwards off-side.

We practised hard to combat this. When we got a free kick in the first-half our plan worked perfectly. I got the ball and scored.

The F.A. match was my first representative appearance— and where better to get such an opportunity than majestic Highbury where this game was played ? I was linked with Portsmouth's Mike Barnard and the other forwards were Eric Parsons (Chelsea), John Atyeo (Bristol City) and Denis Hatsell (Preston).

Now, how did I join Liverpool ?

I was invited to join them while playing at a local cricket ground. Mr. Welsh came along and asked me to come to Anfield as an amateur.

Everton and Bolton suddenly became interested, but I had always had a soft spot for Liverpool—although I was a Rugby League fanatic—and I accepted their offer.

I stayed amateur for a couple of months and was then asked to turn professional. My father thought it a good chance . . . but mother wasn't so keen. She's changed her mind since.

After playing through the " A " and " B " teams, I got into the reserves when Billy Liddell was chosen for Scotland and Mervyn Jones deputised for him.

Liddell was playing so steadily that there seemed no chance of my getting a regular first team place. In the 1954/5 season, however, the opportunity came when Liddell was switched to centre-forward.

Now I hope to qualify for a Football Association coaching certificate. The first course I attended was controlled by Mr. Walter Winterbottom, and famous stars like Joe Mercer and Ivor Broadis gave instruction.

I learned a lot from them and spent many happy hours listening to the stories they had accumulated from years in the game.

Roy Saunders
Liverpool
says

Those pre-match talks are NOT a waste of time

Certainly on one occasion they paid off with a surprise cup win over Everton.

IS pre-match planning a good thing? Most clubs have tactical talks before a game, but there are still folk who do not consider this necessary.

I think it is vital that players get together and have a thorough briefing. If you have some ideas about opponents' weaknesses and strong points, then you go on to the field feeling more confident.

The best example of the use of tactical talks I have known, came in a cup-tie against Everton in 1955. We were not given a chance before this tussle which had set all Merseyside fans arguing.

Everton were doing well in the First Division . . . . we were not doing too brilliantly in Division Two. For some days beforehand our manager, Mr. Don Welsh, had us practising a special move.

He had noticed that when a free kick was taken against them, the Everton defenders moved forward to play the opposing forwards offside.

We arranged that wing half Geoff Twentyman would take the free kicks on his side of the field, and that inside-forward Johnny Evans would lie back.

Well, we got a free kick and the plan went into action. Geoff put his free kick beautifully over the Everton defenders as they moved up. At the same time Evans ran forward and was unchallenged as he got the ball to work an easy opening from which Alan A'Court scored.

I'm certain that goal demoralised Everton . . . . and was the key in our surprise 4—0 win.

Talking of cup-ties brings me to my debut for Liverpool's senior side. It was on January 10, 1952. How do I know the date?—Well, any footballer can recall his first big opportunity and this was certainly mine.

It was an F.A. cup-tie at Gateshead We thought we would beat the Third

Division side without trouble but they sprang a surprise on us and I was a miserable youngster when we lost 1—0.

I was in and out of the side during the rest of the season but a tremendous thrill came when, in April, I was told that I was included among the touring party going to America and Canada.

A tour like this, although a little tiring, is one of the really wonderful things about football. Had I not become a professional I doubt whether I would have ever got to the States.

Certainly I would not have been able to travel in luxurious style aboard two of the ocean " Queens."

As we did not lose one of the ten games played, it is not difficult to imagine just how happy we were on the trip.

But I am forgetting to tell you how I joined Liverpool. As a teenager, I played with a Salford (Lancs) junior team, and was surprised when Mr. Harry Chapman, a Hull scout, asked me if I would like to go to Boothferry Park.

I went for a trial, signed as an amateur, and managed to win a reserve place—and also got into the England youth side which won a European competition.

Hull were anxious for me to stay with them, but it was a long way from home, so I decided to pack my bags. Before I did so, my employer told me he had contacts in Liverpool, and would try to get me fixed up with the club there.

I was soon signed as a part-time professional at Anfield, and was very happy about this as it meant I could still live at home.

I remained as a part-timer for a spell, but eventually decided that to make a real success, I had to give all my time to Soccer.

Quickly, I found the benefit of full-

time training. My confidence improved and certainly I was encouraged by the cheerful companions I had, Les Melville, of Everton, and Tommy McNulty, of Liverpool, who also journey from Manchester each day.

When I was fighting to win a regular place in the side, I had an unfortunate collision with team-mate Bobby Paisley. Bobby is a chunky chap and we collided when going for the ball. Result . . . . my nose was broken in several places and Paisley needed a number of stitches.

It was a sad blow for us all when we were relegated in 1954. Bad luck seemed to be against us all the time; we lost numerous matches by a single goal, and even the signing of a number of new players did not prevent the dreaded drop into Division Two.

But I've no doubt we'll all achieve our ambition to see Liverpool back in the First Division soon. We've just got to get there to please our fans.

Of the players I have met I would like to mention Don Revie and Tommy Taylor especially. Don is my idea of the perfect inside-man—always on the move and drifting into the open space.

Taylor, I consider the best header in the game.

" Don't go falling down and getting your things dirty—mother's coming on Monday and I want a light wash ! "

LIVERPOOL

BACK ROW—Molyneux, Wheeler, Younger, Hughes, Moran, Campbell.
FRONT ROW—Jackson, Rowley, Liddell, Evans, A'Court.

By
*LOUIS
BIMPSON*
of
Liverpool

THEY SOAKED WITH THEIR BOOTS ON !

I 'VE seen some strange and funny sights in my football career but the oddest of them all occurred in St. Louis when I was touring America and Canada with Liverpool, in June, 1953.

For a match in which I wasn't playing, the kick-off was 7 o'clock at night. It was tremendously hot—well over ninety degrees—and I felt as if I was in a furnace merely sitting on the touchline.

The eleven who were playing must have lost pounds in weight, and they looked a sorry sight—hardly able to walk off the field—when the final whistle blew.

I let them get into the dressing-room then joined them. What a sight I saw !

There were eleven red-shirted Liverpool players standing under ice-cold showers—in boots, stockings, shorts and jerseys !

They were so hot and worn out that they just hadn't the strength to take off their kit.

I was unlucky to break my ankle on that tour when we played the Irish international touring team. That accident apart, it was a wonderful trip.

We went out in the " Queen Mary " and returned in the " Queen Elizabeth." We had many happy times on land, but I think those days at sea were the most pleasurable.

In New York we stayed at the big Paramount Hotel for two weeks. Each player got a daily dollar allowance and we were allowed to go and buy meals wherever we wished.

Life seemed to start only as the evening hours approached. Never have I seen a place spring to life so suddenly as did New York when darkness fell.

Most of our travelling was done by 'plane because of the great distances—we had long flights to Montreal, Chicago and Toronto.

My main football days started with Burscough, a Lancashire team near St. Helens. They had spotted me playing with a small club in a local medal competition and I had about two years with them before going in the Army.

Stationed in Austria, I got quite a lot of football, but there was one match, against the British Army touring team, when I didn't see much of the ball.

Opposing me was a big Welsh lad—John Charles. When I now hear people talk of his great ability my mind often goes back to that game.

As demob neared I did not think of football as a full-time career. I anticipated spending my life as a mechanic, with Soccer thrown in at week-ends.

But in January, 1953, eight months after leaving the Forces, I was bound for the big Anfield ground. Apparently, Liverpool had followed up a scout's report and had watched me a couple of times.

We played their "A" team, winning 6-0, and this decided the manager, Don Welsh, to sign me.

A month after changing clubs I was chosen for Liverpool's first team in a friendly match with Burnley. I got all three goals in this game. Burnley must be my lucky club for I hit four in a match against them the following season.

In all, I played only eight senior matches that season but among them was a vital one—our last match with Chelsea, which was to decide whether or not we were relegated.

We had to win both points to be certain we did not go down. In the days beforehand the dressing-room was full of tension as we wondered whether we could pull through.

We just made it by 2-0, Bill Jones getting the first goal and I the second. And so we ended two points

better than Stoke City, who did drop to Division II.

Unfortunately, it was only a season's reprieve for us.

We got off to a bad start in 1953-4, later refound our confidence, and then a tragic accident hit us in a match against Manchester United.

Full-back Eddie Spicer went into a tackle and didn't get up. He had broken a leg.

He was a great clubman and the injury was felt by everyone in the team.

I think we might have turned the corner but for that. Although Dave Underwood, Geoff Twentyman, John Evans and Frank Lock were signed later, our position had reached a critical stage and we could not pull clear.

Even our roaring fans couldn't shake us into life. That proves how we were struggling, for the boys on the Anfield terraces are usually a tremendous help.

I have never heard anything like the enthusiasm of the Spion Kop crowd and many times, when I have flagged, they have spurred me on. But in that relegation season of 1953-4 even they could not help us.

Although Liverpool signed me as a centre-forward, I am a bit of a wanderer. Left-wing, inside-left, inside-right and outside, centre-half and left-half in the reserves—I've been in the lot.

So long as I can keep in the first team I don't mind the changing round, although I do not think it helps one to strike top form.

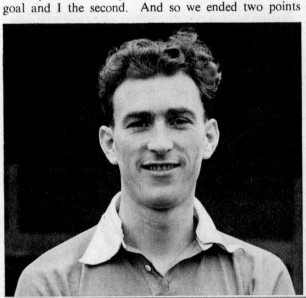

JOHN EVANS (above) and GEOFF TWENTYMAN (right) joined Liverpool when the team was fighting relegation. The move was too late to save the club, who went down.

TONY ROWLEY

ALAN A'COURT

JOHN WHEELER

JIMMY MELIA

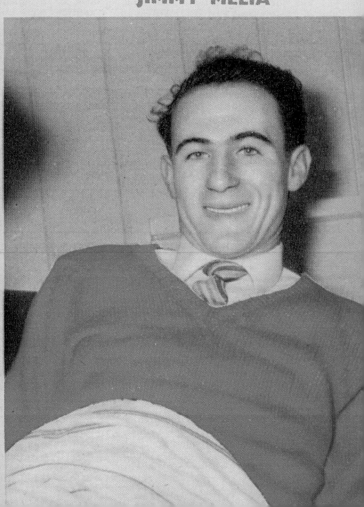

JOHN
MOLYNEUX

RON MORAN
Liverpool

◀ Gift Book 1958–59 | Gift Book 1960–61 ▲

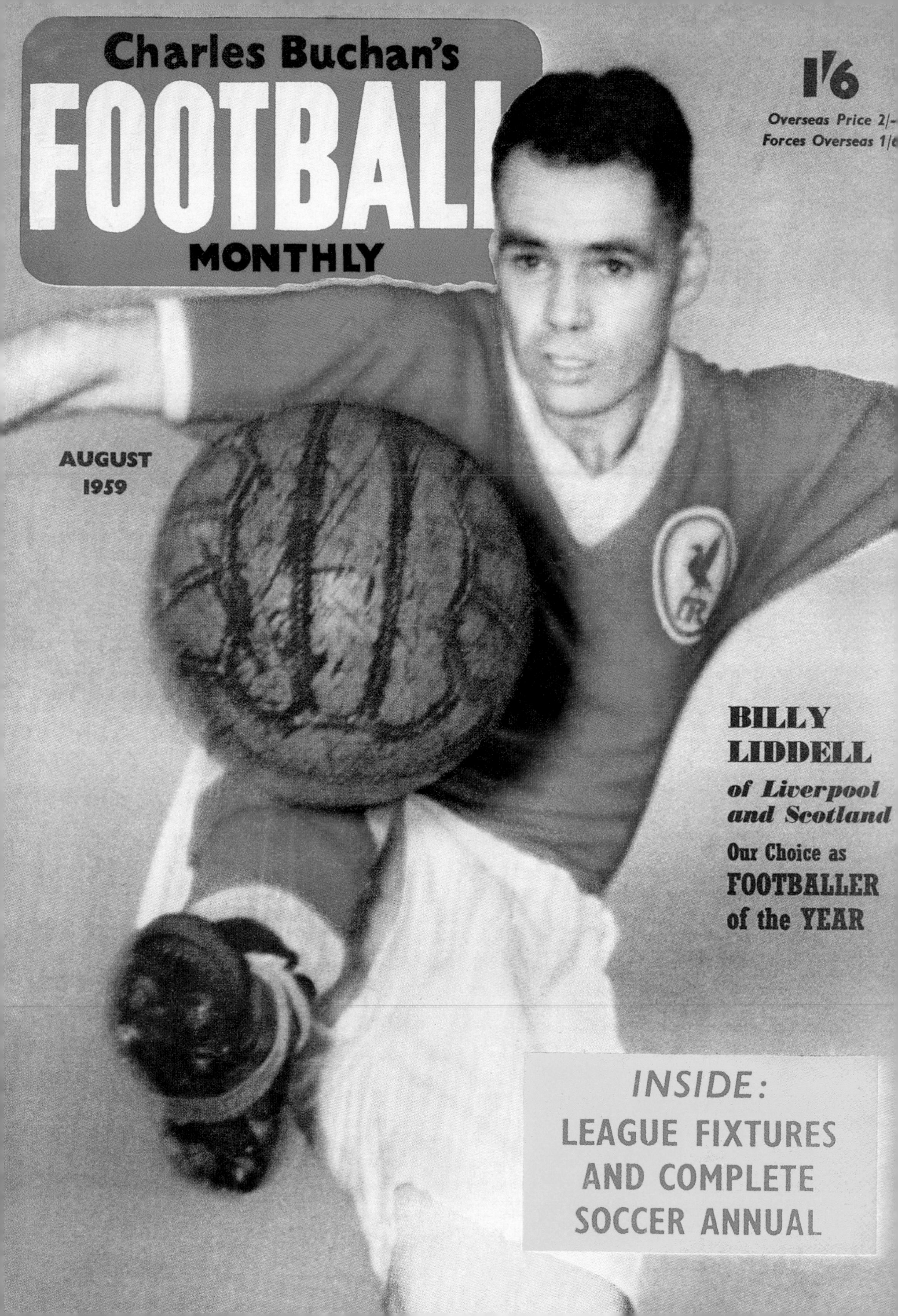

Charles Buchan's FOOTBALL MONTHLY

1'6
Overseas Price 2/-
Forces Overseas 1/6

AUGUST 1959

BILLY LIDDELL
of Liverpool and Scotland

Our Choice as
FOOTBALLER of the YEAR

INSIDE:
LEAGUE FIXTURES
AND COMPLETE
SOCCER ANNUAL

CHARLES BUCHAN'S SELECTION AS
FOOTBALLER of the YEAR

BILLY LIDDELL
Liverpool and Scotland

BILLY LIDDELL, Scotland and Liverpool outside-left, is a man of many interests. Not only is he one of the greatest forwards in the Soccer world, but he is a qualified accountant, a Justice of the Peace and, in his spare time, a big coaching help to Soccer-minded youths.

Since he joined Liverpool as a fifteen-year-old boy from Lochgelly Violet in 1937, Billy has developed a style of his own, fast, direct and powerful. His one object is either to make goals for his colleagues or score them himself.

He is blessed with a fine physique—height 5 ft. 10½ in., weight 12 st. 10 lb.—and, once in possession of the ball, is a hard man to tackle, a man with a purpose.

Liddell gained his first Scottish cap in 1942 and had the distinction of playing for the Great Britain team that trounced the Rest of Europe 6—1 at Hampden Park in 1947.

He is the complete footballer, at home in any position in the forward line. His effectiveness in front of goal with either foot has brought many goals for his club and country.

Born in Dunfermline, Billy, after 22 years of valuable service to Liverpool, may be nearing the end of a wonderful career. But he still remains a model for every sporting youth in the country.

FOOTBALL MON

VISITS

LIVERPOOL

JOHN WHEELER

BERT SLATER

ALAN A'COURT

JOHN MOLYNEUX

DICK WHITE

GERRY BYRNE

DAVE HICKSON

JIMMY HARROWER

Another week-end spoiled! Johnny Hills (right), of Bristol Rovers, has deflected a shot by Jimmy Melia, of Liverpool, into his own goal.

▲ Gift Book 1962–63

SECOND DIVISION CHAMPIONS

LIVERPOOL

Standing—Milne, Yeats, Furnell, Moran, Byrne, Leishman. Sitting—Callaghan, Hunt, Ian St. John (with club mascot), Melia, A'Court.

▲ August 1962

Charles Buchan's
FOOTBALL
MONTHLY

JULY, 1962

1/6

Overseas
price 2/-
Forces
overseas 1/6

TOMMY LEISHMAN and **GORDON MILNE** Liverpool

YOU HAVE TO BE KEEN

THEY say that if you want to succeed at Soccer you must often make sacrifices. Things don't always go easy for you when you are struggling to make the grade, but enthusiasm can carry you a long way. Take my word for it, I know.

I had always hoped that I would be a good player when I was a tall, gangling boy in my native Aberdeen. At first, it seemed fairly easy. I represented my school, then Aberdeen boys and Scotland boys at centre-half.

I had little chance to watch big Soccer—I was always too busy playing. Then I left school—and suddenly it wasn't so easy.

My first job was as an apprentice slaughterman with a local butcher. I used to start at four o'clock in the morning and finish at nine o'clock. The work was sheer hard labour—especially for a growing lad.

I was serving this arduous apprenticeship when I began playing in junior Soccer with Aberdeen Lads. Still a centre-half, I thought I was heading for the big-time when I was spotted by a Celtic scout. But the weeks went by and I gave up hope. I imagined he had forgotten me.

Much later, I heard that the scout had been involved in a bad car crash while on his way back to Glasgow to give his report about me to manager Jimmy McGrory. That unfortunate scout was in hospital a long time and, naturally, his report on my play was forgotten. So, instead of becoming a Celtic player I was picked up by Dundee United, then in the Scottish Second Division, and under the managership of Mr. Jerry Kerr.

I had four seasons with United, and helped them to promotion. My game was improving, and I felt that I really had a chance of bigger things, particularly when I was picked as reserve for Scotland against Wales and Ireland, and as reserve for the Scottish Under-23 team who played England.

By then, I had been called up for National Service in the Army. I was stationed at Aldershot and there played in the Army side with Johnny Byrne and Alec Young.

Things became tough again at this stage. I have never done so much travelling in my life—and I hope I never will again.

I helped the Second Training Battalion of the R.A.S.C. to win the Army Cup (we had reached the Final the previous year), and every week-end I flew to Scotland to play for Dundee United.

The routine was this. I had to make my way by train and bus to London airport and from there by plane to Glasgow. After that there was a two-hour train journey to Dundee, which I would reach either very late Friday night or early Saturday morning.

I would usually cover the long journey back to Aldershot by bus and train. And I quite often travelled up again for a mid-week game in Scotland. Believe me . . . I grew to *hate* the sight and sound of trains!

But I must say, I owed a lot to the grand co-operation of my C.O., Colonel J. Dagham. I hope I have repaid him in some way by making good at my chosen profession.

I had no idea that Liverpool were interested in me until they came to sign me in July, 1961. In fact, I thought they were about to sign Tony Knapp, who was then with Leicester City.

One week-end in the summer of 1961, I had gone home to Aberdeen for a short leave. On Saturday night I got a telegram asking me to meet Dundee United officials in an Edinburgh hotel the following day. I had no idea what it was all about.

When I reached the North British Hotel there were Dundee United manager, Mr. Kerr, Liverpool manager Bill Shankly and some of his directors. Bill Shankly—a great talker, Bill, and a fellow Scot—soon convinced me that my future was with the "Reds" at Anfield. "You'll be going to a club booked for promotion," he told me.

Of course, Bill was right and in April, 1962, I was acting skipper of the Liverpool side which *did* return to the First Division after an absence of eight years.

I have no regrets about trying my luck in English Soccer. And if there is a better crowd of loyal fans in the country than those at Anfield, then I would like to meet them.

Since I began playing regularly in the English League—and I was almost an ever-present last season—I have been surprised by the number of good players I have come up against, and also the high standard of football produced by top and bottom clubs.

There is a much greater gap in Scotland, where the bottom-of-the-table clubs are well below the class of the leaders. And few of the leading Scottish Second Division clubs can hope for more than a mid-table placing should they win promotion to the First Division.

It is very different in England and I believe that most of my fellow Anglo-Scots share my views.

One of the toughest and best centre-forwards I had to try to stop during Liverpool's promotion run was Leyton Orient's Dave Dunmore. To my surprise, he had apparently failed to make the grade with Tottenham or West Ham. Yet I rate him a great player.

He gave me a terrific battle when we drew 3—3 with the Orient at Anfield. Orient shocked us—we didn't realise how good they were!

Orient also held us to a draw on their own ground later in the season when a point was precious to both clubs. Orient were by far the better side that day and they deserved to go up with us.

▲ October 1962

RONNIE YEATS
Liverpool

LIVERPOOL

5 times champions ... makers of history ... and the scene of incessant 'tribal war' with Everton

by Geoffrey Green

The character of great clubs is formed by the atmosphere of the district in which they play, and by the spirit of those who support them.

Britain's most distinguished football writer captures that character. The subject this time: Liverpool.

MERSEYSIDE does not care to live on the side of mercy. The tides of enthusiasm that sweep the city of Liverpool are far too strong.

It is a straight alternative for those who dare to challenge those waters: live or die. And those who presume to tread the waves more often than not are sunk.

It is a natural birthright. Just as the two great clubs—Everton and Liverpool—of this teeming, powerful waterfront, decorated by ocean liners, giant shipyards and a striving industrial community, unite to withstand the onset of others, so they easily split in personal rivalry, a family divided against itself in implacable enmity.

The choice is clear cut. There can be no half-way house. You are either one or the other: either Everton or Liverpool, symbols of a ceaseless tribal war over the years.

Its echoes are to be found in the Rangers and Celtic, of Glasgow; in the Wednesday and United, of Sheffield; in the United and City, of Manchester; in Arsenal and Tottenham, of North London. Yet on

Merseyside it somehow seems all the fiercer, more relentless. The reason, I suppose, lies in the very roots of the matter.

Anfield, the present home of Liverpool, was originally used by Everton in 1884 until the "Toffeemen" moved across the city to Goodison Park in 1892.

Thus Anfield, with its towering, hump-backed Spion Kop, and its record crowd of 61,905 for a Cup-tie with Wolverhampton Wanderers in 1952, may rightly regard itself as the first setting for senior football on Merseyside.

Yet it is there that the argument splits—

Everton or Liverpool, which the greater?

It is the argument of two religions that have emerged from a common stem.

Liverpool, in fact, were founded as a new club in 1892 by John McKenna, later president of the Football League.

Its first pillars were a handful of Everton members who, spurning the move to Goodison, remained at Anfield.

And from that moment in 1893 when they were first elected to the Second Division they have remained in the limelight one way or another.

It was Tom Watson, the late secretary, who perhaps struck the note best when he once said:

"Our life at Liverpool is full of trouble. We are always either fighting for Championships, Cups or promotion; or else we are fighting to escape relegation."

Well, at least life has been full for them: "life's tapering candle" as the poet wrote. And now again in this season of 1962-63 the flame is spurting up once more.

They are adding their warmth to that of Everton to make Merseyside a vibrant, dangerous stretch.

Nor is it to be wondered at, for they have just emerged from a traumatic spell of seven years from the season 1954 when they found themselves elbowed back into the Second Division.

From then until last spring, when at last they climbed the ladder of promotion, they lived through a searing spate of near-misses.

In successive seasons they ended third, third, fourth, fourth, third and then third again, until finally they shook off the dust of the Second Division.

It might have broken the spirit of others. But not Liverpool.

It is the tremendous enthusiasm on Merseyside that strikes one. It is always the same, through thick and thin, a worthy reflection of a hardy community that can look at either wealth or poverty with an equal, unflinching eye.

Perhaps it is the salt of the nearby sea in their veins: perhaps the small injection of happy-go-lucky blarney in their midst, offered by immigrants across the Irish Sea, the noisy, boisterous element of the "Liverpool Irish".

Whatever it is, the feeling hits you like the blast of a furnace, like the sharp threat of a sword drawn from its scabbard.

And when Liverpool come face to face with Everton, either at Anfield or Goodison, it is wiser for outsiders to keep far away from the argument. The affair is far too private and deep-rooted.

However, I did once pluck up courage to

ELISHA SCOTT ... of immortal goalkeeping fame.

▲ April 1963

LIVERPOOL

intrude at a respectable distance. It was an F.A. Cup semi-final at neutral Maine Road, Manchester. The year was 1950. Liverpool beat Everton 3—0 on that occasion to reach Wembley for their first and only time.

But that was not so much the point for me. All these years later I can still almost hear the deep baying of that 75,000 crowd. It seemed a different note to any other I had heard: deeper, more fanatical. It sounded like some giant religious persecution.

At one end were the red decorated rattles of Liverpool, at the other the blue of Everton.

They swirled incessantly and though they looked like dragon-fly wings glittering in the sunlight they sounded like the deafening machine-guns of a battle on the Somme.

It is a fierce enthusiasm and a fierce argument that is rooted in time itself. Whatever Everton can boast, Liverpool may answer almost word for word.

True, the F.A. Cup itself has never gone to Anfield, but at least Liverpool can point to five League championship titles when the prize of the First Division has graced their mantelpiece.

They can point to some unusual feats, too. In 1905 and 1906, in successive seasons, they won the Second and First Division crowns. That had not been done before. It took Everton 26 years and Tottenham Hotspur 45 to equal that achievement.

Then there is their League record of the longest run without defeat: 31 matches from the start of the 1893-94 season to the third game of 1894-95, including victory in a promotion Test match of those far-off days.

I have said Liverpool have never won the Cup. Yet here again they have found themselves in a part of history. The first of their two Finals came at the old Crystal Palace in 1914. Burnley won 1—0, but for the first time a reigning monarch graced the occasion.

King George V took his place in the Royal Box and to honour an all-Lancashire affair he wore a red rose in his buttonhole.

That was a turning point for football, socially. It set a precedent in fashionable circles which has since been followed and, indeed, widened.

Once upon a time Liverpool were known as a team of "Macs" with a strong Scottish flavour, even though John McKenna used to say that it needed the wealth of Croesus, and a shipyard thrown in, to entice the Scots to Anfield.

Yet basically, as befits a seaport community, Liverpool have a broad cosmopolitan background.

Who can forget Gordon Hodgson and Nieuwenhuys, known as "Nivvy" to the terraces, two great South African footballers? There was the immortal Elisha Scott, Ireland's goalkeeper. J. E. Doig and Alec Raisbec represented the earlier Scottish clans, later followed by Billy Liddell, Scotland's outside-left for so long and one of the greatest gentlemen the game has ever

BILLY LIDDELL . . . a gentleman and a loyal servant to the game.

known. A loyal servant indeed, he was rightly elected a Justice of the Peace, and in 1957-58 surpassed Elisha Scott's record of 433 League match appearances.

The stylish, polished Bromilow, Ephraim Longworth, and Harry Chambers were a distinguished English trio of internationals after the First World War, followed in more recent decades by Phil Taylor, Stubbins, Hughes and Alan A'Court (still playing), the last two of whom wore an England shirt in the World Cups of 1950 and 1958.

So the long parade of the years passes. But the enthusiasm and the fire of Anfield lives on.

GERRY BYRNE
Liverpool and England

▲ June 1963

CHARLES BUCHAN'S

FOOTBALL

MONTHLY

The World's Greatest Soccer Magazine

MAY, 1963

AN ST. JOHN
of Scotland

RON MORAN

KEVIN LEWIS

2/-
OVERSEAS
PRICE 2/6
FORCES
OVERSEAS 2/-

RON YEATS

STARS of LIVERPOOL

by IAN ST. JOHN
Liverpool and Scotland

Ian St. John presented to Prince Philip before the England—Scotland match in 1961.

THERE'S NO NOISE

ALTHOUGH I am a centre-forward I don't score goals quite as often as some of the other fellows in the same line of business. I am sure I will never be in line for a goal-scoring record, club or otherwise.

But that doesn't worry me, for goal-making, even more than goal-scoring, is my job at Liverpool.

When I moved from Scottish to English Soccer two years ago it meant not only a switch of club and country . . . I also had to change my game, by order. And I must say I have been delighted with it all.

As soon as I had signed for Liverpool, the "Boss", Mr. Bill Shankly, told me I could forget the orthodox spearhead game I had been playing for Motherwell.

At Anfield, he said, he wanted me to move around and try to create openings for the other forwards. And so in two seasons I have played as an inside-forward in the centre.

It suits me fine—just so long as somebody is getting the goals. It is a more satisfying game to play, for I am

not so dependent on others. This way I can look for work and put more into the game, rather than stay upfield waiting for things to be laid on for me.

The change was not hard to make, for I played at inside-forward in schools and youth football, and for my junior club, Douglas Water Thistle. I had to . . . I was too small to be considered as a centre-forward.

I wish I had been blessed with a few extra inches in height; there are a lot of good centres I can remember that would have been turned to better advantage. Yet I played the spearhead at Fir Park . . . and at 5 ft. 7½ in. I was just about the tallest Motherwell forward!

We had a bonny side there, and I had some grand players around me. Fellows like George Hunter, Andy Weir and Pat Quinn, now with Blackpool, and with Bert McCann behind us at wing-half. They played some great stuff.

There was another change I found when I moved to England—the attitude of supporters.

Good as the Motherwell side was, the Fir Park fans

▲ Gift Book 1963–64

seldom seemed to be satisfied. We played some really attractive stuff, but it was more appreciated, I always thought, elsewhere. Our fans were a hard lot to please.

What a difference at Anfield! True, we were winning, and gained promotion to the First Division in my first season—and didn't do too badly last season—but I have found my English supporters much more appreciative—and encouraging.

Of course, the Anfield crowd are something apart when it comes to supporting their team. They are terrific, compelling you always to go all out. I lap up the intense, boisterous blast when the Anfield crowd goes full out on lung power. Everything seems to mean so much more.

But I have found it, or something like it, on other English grounds—at White Hart Lane and Old Trafford. At Goodison Park, too, for very obvious reasons, when our two clubs meet.

Back home you would hear a comparable din only at Parkhead and Ibrox . . . and, of course, the cheers were seldom for you and your side. If you did have many fans at such games you wouldn't hear them . . . not with those Celtic and Rangers fans in full chorus.

Another big difference I have found in moving is in coaching and preparation.

I was a part-timer at Fir Park, except for my last two seasons there. I worked out my apprenticeship as a fitter—Bobby Kennedy, of Manchester City, worked for the same firm, and he was also an old rival in schools football.

As a part-timer, like most of the rest, it was a case of

IAN ST. JOHN . . . he likes looking for work.

LIKE THE ANFIELD NOISE
—and I love it!

two training nights a week and meeting the team only on match-days. Tactical talks, standard practice in England, were unknown . . . you went out and played your game and hoped it would tie up with the rest.

"Live, eat and sleep" this game, they tell you. But that is possible only in England, where managers and coaches are always at hand, where players are always together and the game is around and about you throughout the week.

I won no school honours to attract attention to myself, although my pals and I had a ball out from morning to night and played almost until we dropped. For me, progress was by way of the Boys' Brigade, boys' club football, and then Douglas Water Thistle. Then I came to Motherwell's notice and joined them at 18.

When I got my first cap for Scotland—against West Germany in 1958—it was because Bobby Kerr, of Kilmarnock, had to cry off through injury. John White, of Spurs, also played his first international that day. The Czechs are the best national side I have played against, and I was not in the least surprised, as

so many were, when they got to the World Cup Final.

For me it seems to have been all excitement since I joined Liverpool, starting with that promotion run from the Second to the First Division.

But for sheer, tingling drama there has been nothing to beat our replayed Fourth Round Cup-tie with Burnley last February. You may remember that we were 1—1, with 30 seconds to go, when Adam Blacklaw drove his clearance against me and I was brought down going round him to push the ball into the empty net.

It was a tragic finish for Adam, who had been terrific that night. When Ronnie Moran came to take the penalty I just couldn't look. I had my eyes closed tight as he ran up. Silly, because a rebound might have come my way.

The next thing I knew was that the heavens were bursting with sound . . . Moran's kick had gone home. I was just limp, and not ashamed to admit that for once my nerves had got the better of me.

CHAMPIONS...YEAH! YEAH! YEAH!

Liverpool had beaten Arsenal 5—0 to take the League title from their neighbours Everton. And this is the reception they got from the "wackers". Manager Bill Shankly acknowledges with a wave.

▲ June 1964

CHARLES BUCHAN'S
FOOTBALL MONTHLY

The World's Greatest Soccer Magazine

JUNE, 1964

ROGER HUNT
England

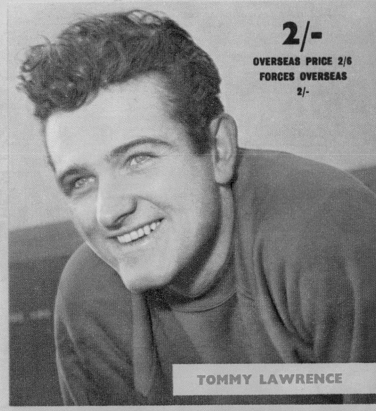

2/-
OVERSEAS PRICE 2/6
FORCES OVERSEAS
2/-

TOMMY LAWRENCE

IAN CALLAGHAN

GORDON MILNE
England

★ STARS OF LIVERPOOL ★

RONNIE YEATS, captain of Liverpool, the Football League champions, answers 21 questions put to him by **JERRY DAWSON**

IT'S FAB,
(y'know, like . . .

Q. WHAT were your feelings when the whistle blew after your game with Arsenal on April 18—and you knew that you were champions?

A. *I FELT my usual relief that the game was over, and that we had won, but when we ran the lap of honour round the ground, well that was like a fairy tale ending.*

That we should clinch the championship on our own ground, before our own fans, was perfect. It reminded me of winning promotion from the Scottish Second Division with Dundee United in 1960.

Q. WAS there a point in the season when you felt that you had a real chance of the title?

A. *YES, after our three victories in the Easter matches. Then we knew that we were in with a big chance. Early in the season it was obvious that, come what may, we had three hard matches over Easter so we tried hard to build up a reserve of points, just in case!*

We never expected to get six points,

but on top of this we "laid" the Leicester bogey, scoring our first goal against them in five matches. I wasn't playing that day (I was under suspension), but it was a great thrill.

Q. CAN you think of any single factor that contributed most towards winning the title?

A. *NOT a single one, but two—team spirit and a brilliant manager! Mr. Shankly's tactics paid off. What a man! Everyone listens to him. He makes you want to play your heart out for him. Yes, I think even the team spirit stemmed from him!*

Q. WAS the season a big strain on you personally? Would you rather not have had the captaincy?

A. *NO! The boys never needed driving. I may have shouted now and then to encourage them, but they all knew their job from the manager's briefing —and just got on with it.*

How from time to time we failed (as against Swansea in the Cup) I'll never know. That's Soccer, I suppose. Good or bad, I had a consistent season, so I had no personal worries.

Q. WHICH was your hardest game of the season?

A. *THEY'VE all been hard, but my three hardest were those in which I didn't play, against Bolton, Tottenham and Leicester at Easter. I watched the Bolton and Leicester games and nearly wore myself out with worry. I just couldn't face the Tottenham game. When I heard we'd won I felt great!*

Q. WHO was the best centre-forward you came up against last season?

A. *I COULDN'T pick out any single one, they all seem to be good when they play against me. I treat them all with the same respect.*

Q. WHICH side had the best forward line, and which side the best defence?

A. *BEST forward line? Definitely Leicester when they beat us 1-0 at Anfield. When we played them at*

Leicester at Easter it seemed to have gone—just not the same line.

Best defence? Our reserve side! And I'm not kidding. We played several practice games against them and we just couldn't do anything right against their defence. They were great!

Q. WHICH has contributed most to winning the title—your attack or defence?

A. *THAT'S a hard one—almost impossible to answer fairly. We shared the load, I suppose. While we finished with the best defensive record in the league, the forwards still had to score to win matches. Defences can only save points—not win them.*

Q. THE old question—which would you rather have won, the F.A. Cup or the League Championship, now that both entail entry into a European competition?

A. *THE League Championship. A side has only to win half-a-dozen games to win the cup. To win the League title shows all-season consistency. Let's face it, you need a lot of luck to win the Cup. We are still a young side. We can win the Cup—with all its glamour—next season!*

Q. HAVE you any plans prepared for the European Cup games?

A. *THAT'S the manager's job. And don't worry—he'll find a plan all right, and a way to beat anyone we play.*

Q. WHAT do you think are your chances of winning this trophy—which no British club has yet done?

A. *WITH that bit of luck necessary in any knock-out competition—we can do it. With Mr. Shankly planning for us, and the Kop rooting for us, we could win the County Cricket Championship too!*

Q. WILL you have to alter the style of the team for the European competition?

A. *DEFINITELY NO! That would be fatal. Any attempt to change what has taken so long to achieve could ruin the side. That doesn't mean to say we always play the same way. Naturally, our match-tactics vary— depending on the opposition.*

BILL SHANKLY
...brilliant manager

▲ June 1964

WACK!
being champions!)

RON YEATS

Q. A LOT of players were suspended last season. Do you think this is because play has become dirtier?

A. *NO—not at all. In fact I've discussed this several time with retired players, and when they tell me what they used to get away with I know that if anything the game is cleaner.*

Q. THEN why have so many been sent-off?

A. *SIMPLY because referees have been clamping down oftener and harder. We are often penalised for things that would have been overlooked a few seasons past.*

Q. WHAT then do you think of present-day referees?

A. *I DON'T think that there are enough absolutely top-class referees who can command respect from the moment they step on the field. There are some of course—and they do get respect. And the games they control are better for it!*

Q. DO YOU think referees generally are too tough?

A. *YES! Some are too ready to whistle for petty fouls. They stop the game far too often—much more than is necessary. And all this spoils it for the spectators just as much as it does for the players.*

Q. WHAT is your opinion of Continental referees?

A. *I'VE only played under them in the Army and almost every one seemed to take a dislike to me. I know I play it hard, but I think my size was against me.*
A little chap playing hard is not quite as devastating as a big chap playing hard. I haven't yet played for Liverpool under a Continental referee. I only hope I don't suffer.

Q. BACK to the game itself. Do you think players should be allowed to play their natural way, or to a plan or system?

A. *AT LIVERPOOL we play to a tactical plan. We don't treat all opponents the same way. This I think is the reason for our success. Yes—it's a plan for me every time.*

Q. WHICH in your opinion is the best of the systems?

A. *ONE in which the centre-forward is a striker. I don't like the 4-2-4 plan unless you have the players who were signed just for this plan.*
It is difficult to play, and just as difficult to play against if it is played correctly.

Q. DO you think that the present wages system is ideal?

A. *YES I think every man has the right to negotiate his own rate of pay to his own satisfaction.*
But where players and management agree, I think it desirable that the leading players should be paid roughly the same. Star payment to star players, sometimes upsets a team.

Q. FINALLY, how do you see your future?

A. *AT LIVERPOOL! I'm happily settled here with my wife and three daughters. They are very happy and I'm with a great club with a great manager—what more can I ask?*
So long as I'm treated as fairly as I have been so far, I can see me ending my days with the best club in the world. LIV-ER-POOL!!!

COVER-PIX

MANAGER BILL SHANKLY refuses to pick between his players when handing out praise—nor does he care for anybody else doing so. To Bill they are all as one—LIVERPOOL. But we have had to be more selective with our front cover; we couldn't get all the Reds at one go.

But even Bill will agree that in picturing goalkeeper Tommy Lawrence, the big cheerful Scot, the England pair, Gordon Milne and Roger Hunt, the local boy Ian Callaghan, we have featured four players who have contributed enormously to the Merseyside club's success.

Lawrence took his chance two seasons ago when injury kept out Jim Furnell, now with Arsenal. Once installed, he made himself a permanent fixture.

Milne, son of the Preston manager, left that club before his Dad took over. That was four years ago. It took time for the Koppites to accept his quiet, thoughtful game . . . now he's an idol and an established England wing-half.

Hunt is recognised as the Anfield goal-merchant. His lean, lithe dash through the middle is a Soccer sight that spells trouble for any defence. He doesn't need two bites at the cherry very often.

Alongside him on the wing is the Liverpool speedster, Callaghan. An England Under-23 cap, he is young and capable enough to win full honours before long.

CHARLES BUCHAN'S
FOOTBALL
MONTHLY

APRIL, 1964

BILLY STEVENSON
Liverpool

play in the style of the 1963/4 champions

champions LIVERPOOL F.C.

wearers of

sportswear

The Choice of Champions

HUMPHREYS BROS. LTD.,
P.O. Box Dept. CB5., Wilmslow, Cheshire.

Club secretaries are invited to apply for the full colour Umbrochure of Sportswear, which also contains the complete range of Adidas sportswear.

▲ September 1964

CHARLES BUCHAN'S
FOOTBALL
MONTHLY

NOVEMBER, 1964

The World's Greatest Soccer Magazine

2/-
OVERSEAS PRICE 2/6
FORCES OVERSEAS
2/-

PETER THOMPSON
Liverpool

LIVERPOOL...!

There's no place like it and no fans like ours on Spion Kop

by GORDON MILNE
Liverpool and England

GORDON MILNE

AS I watch my year-old son, Andrew, bracing himself to take his first, faltering steps, I wonder if the football tradition in the Milne family will be carried on somewhere around the nineteen-eighties.

Andrew as a Christian name? That's the Scots blood in the family making itself heard. My mum and dad are Scottish, but I arrived when my father was playing for Preston, so I am English by birth. I dare say quite a few of my ancestors have "taken a turn" since I pulled the white shirt of the Auld Enemy over my head.

Preston, at about the time I came on the scene, was a virtual hame from hame for Scots like my dad. Look at North End's Cup Final team of 1937—the one beaten by Sunderland . . .

There were EIGHT Scots in that side . . . Gallimore, Andy Beattie, Bill Shankly—my present Liverpool boss and one of my father's greatest friends—Dougal, Frank O'Donnell, his brother Hugh, Fagan and my father.

A year later, when a sensational last second penalty by George Mutch beat Huddersfield, there were NINE Scots in the Preston side. Dad was missing, put out of action by a Fifth Round injury at Highbury.

So here I am, the son of a Scottish footballing-father, born almost in North End's goalmouth, brought up in a school which backed onto the Deepdale ground. You can understand why I wonder if my young Andrew, like his father and grandad, will follow the same Soccer trail.

It was the best thing that has happened to me so far in my career when I left Preston for Liverpool . . . meaning no disrespect to North End. I could not have been comfortable at a club where I was a player and my father the manager. I hadn't been happy when he was made trainer while I was on the staff.

I know this father-and-son tie-up has happened before, but I don't think it works, particularly when the fierce, full glare of publicity is turned on you for almost every waking minute.

I don't see how father and son could be absolutely neutral about the many issues that can crop up in "the family" which is a football club. For instance, the question of whether or not the son is as good as the father believes would be only one of the possible arguments.

For such reasons I was happy when in 1960 Liverpool came for me. Since then there have been many other reasons to cause me to look back on that day and think myself lucky to be at Anfield, for the Reds are a big club in every way.

My transfer to Liverpool was quite a boost to my morale, for on the August evening I signed I had been sitting in the stands at Deepdale watching my North End pals against Arsenal. After only three games for Preston at the start of the new season I had been dropped!

I didn't know, as I watched, that the Liverpool "boss", Mr. Shankly, was looking on, but the business of settling the transfer was quickly wrapped up after the match. Cliff Britton, then Preston's manager, and Dad thought it would be a good move for me, but I didn't need any urging . . . I jumped at the chance.

The next night I was in action for Liverpool, playing before the Spion Koppites against Southampton. It was

▲ Gift Book 1964–65

quite an experience, believe me. I have a lot for which to thank my old club. I had come up through the junior ranks, having played for Preston and Lancashire Boys sides, but I stayed as a part-timer until I was 21, to serve my time as a joiner.

Most of my early League games were as deputy to Tommy Docherty; I became a regular only after he was transferred to Arsenal.

Tommy and Tom Finney were generous with their advice to me. Great sportsmen! They knew of the struggles and the trials of others and passed on the benefit of their experience. Nor must I forget Willie Cunningham. This grand club-servant "fathered" me in many games, roaring out advice and encouragement throughout a match.

Last season the crowds improved at Deepdale. That gave me almost as much pleasure as my own club's success, for I was happy that my father was leading the old club to better days.

Still, there's no place like Liverpool. Nowhere else is there anything like the fanatical support to drive a team on. The fans keep you going when you feel like dropping.

This inspiration has made me—I hope—a better player because of the urgency and determination it has helped to put into my game.

This, with the help and team-work of a great bunch of fellows, stepped up my game to the point where in May last year I got my England chance against Brazil.

It was a good time to get into the England line-up, for at that time all the boys were hitting it off. I don't have to tell you what that first cap—and the others which followed—meant to me.

As a kid, I was brought up as much on football stories as the nursery kind. I lapped them up.

Now my young Andrew has a lot to hear from HIS dad. My hope is that the day will come when he can carry on the family tradition. I'm looking forward to buying him his first football boots!

JIMMY MILNE

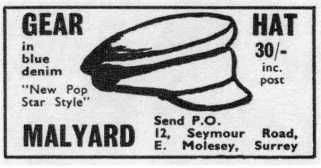
▲ Selected from 1963-65

EE-AYE-ADDIO!

▲ June 1965

It's their Cup, Liverpool's, after the third time of trying, and left is The Queen giving it to skipper Ron Yeats. Above, those who won it—Back row: Yeats, Milne (who did not play because he was injured), Stevenson, St. John, Lawler, Byrne, Front: Lawrence, Thompson, Strong, Smith, Hunt, Callaghan. And below, manager Bill Shankly.

F.A. CUP FINAL
LIVERPOOL 2, LEEDS 1
(Hunt, St. John)   (Bremner)
Attendance: 100,000. Receipts: £89,000.

ON a day demanding their greatest effort Leeds were found woefully wanting. Liverpool, by their domination of the second half, should not have let the match run into the first extra-time Final for 18 years.

Valiant defence alone kept Leeds in the game. Their attack died early and never—Bremner's goal apart—disturbed the assured Liverpool control. Stevenson, who took over as the general provider for his side, was the man of the match.

Byrne showed magnificent spirit. He broke a collar-bone in the early minutes but played on. He, with Smith, Strong—deputising for Milne—Lawler, Yeats and Stevenson gave Lawrence the most idle Final any goalkeeper has had.

Sprake did wonders for Leeds. Charlton stood up under the incessant Liverpool pressure, but Collins could not find a spark of form, or infuse the authority his side had enjoyed in the rest of the season.

It was too one-sided to be a Final to remember. On the wings, Thompson and Callaghan, and with St. John working like a beaver in the middle, Liverpool called the tune after a dull opening. Two headers by Hunt and St. John eventually gained them the victory which should have come much earlier.

Liverpool: Lawrence; Lawler, Byrne; Strong, Yeats, Stevenson; Callaghan, Hunt, St. John, Smith, Thompson.
Leeds: Sprake; Reaney, Bell; Bremner, Charlton, Hunter; Giles, Storrie, Peacock, Collins, Johanneson.

LIVERPOOL: Back row—Gordon Milne
Front—Ian Calla

yrne, Tommy Lawrence, Chris Lawler, Ron Yeats, Billy Stevenson.

ger Hunt, Ian St. John, Tommy Smith, Peter Thompson.

KEN DODD

gets his
buck
teeth out
of his
jam
butty
to say
of
soccer ...

Dodd shows Liverpool stars how to train—and that really WAS a laugh!

TATTYPHILARIOUS!

Dodd and friend (Dodd on the left).

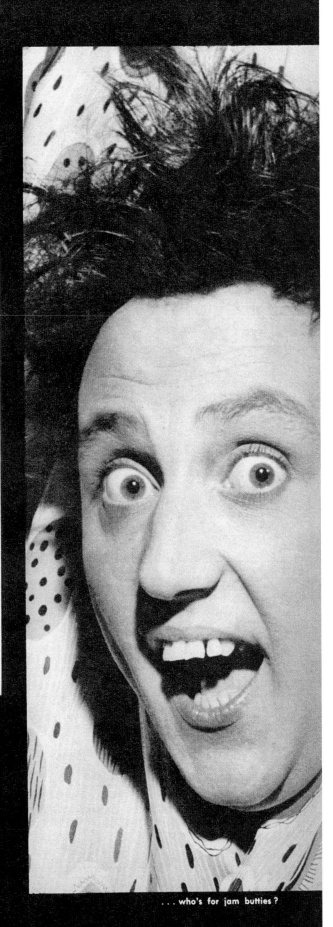

I'D like to say how tickled I h'am to be writing about my favourite sport—but first a few words about football.

I've always been keen on football because of my dad. He was a red-hot Liverpudlian, and when I was a young boy he made me wear a little red jersey—and hung me in the rear window of the family car!

In those days I couldn't afford to watch either Liverpool or Everton, and every Saturday afternoon found me on the terraces at the Knotty Ash Stadium—price of admittance, two empty lemonade bottles, or a piece of stale cake for the chairman!

But seriously—the first Soccer game I ever saw was when an uncle took me to Anfield when I was four years old to watch Liverpool play Everton. I don't remember much about it—but I've been a Liverpool fan ever since.

And I *do* remember that my uncle was a very proud man that day—my auntie was playing left-back for Everton! He was chock full of plumptiousness!

As a boy I played inside-right for my school, Holt High School, Liverpool, but when I left it was the end of my playing career, chiefly because of my prominent teeth. I was scared stiff of breaking them.

They are an asset today, of course. In fact, I'm the only member of our family who can eat tomatoes through the strings of a tennis racquet. When I was a baby, my mother thought my milk teeth were coming in bottles—and I often get fan letters from buck rabbits!

Back to the point: the fact that I was no longer playing

.. and Liverpool would want £20 a week OFF him to let him play for them!

... who's for jam butties?

Two "mokes" with one thought—how did this chap get into our act?

in Saturday Soccer meant that I had more time to watch Liverpool—which was all right by me, and still is.

And one of the reasons why I'm such a keen follower of Liverpool is because of the wonderful atmosphere at Anfield Road on match days—thousands of fans singing on the Kop—and me behind the goal wearing me red and white singlet!

My only complaint is that I can't watch anything like the number of games I want to. Every time I'm at home I seem to be reporting to the probation officer!

We always have Saturday matinees when I'm in Liverpool, and I am hardly ever able to watch night matches. But I do watch them when I'm between shows—and I am not exactly a stranger to Anfield on training days.

On these days I often talk tactics to Bill Shankly, and when I put forward my plans to beat opposing defences Bill gets really worked up. In fact, he gets so excited that he often falls-off—to sleep!

But I still act as a sort of unofficial scout for the Reds—the result of a conversation I had in 1958 with the then manager Phil Taylor.

We were discussing the need to develop young players—and as I spend a lot of my spare time watching schoolboy and junior games, I arranged to tip him off if I saw anyone who showed promise.

I haven't yet discovered a Billy Liddell or an Ian St. John, but I still keep my eyes open. And if you are thinking of questioning my qualifications for the job, well, a lot of people who saw me play as a schoolboy said I had a great potential— so I went on a diet.

And I've had a varied experience of the game. I first played for St. Agnes's School for Young Gentlewomen—till they found me out. Then I had my hair cut and played for Holt High School for Boys! After a few games the sports master told me I'd make a good comedian—so I took his advice. There's no time for gertitude in Soccer!

One of Soccer's show-piece games that I have not yet seen is the F.A. Cup Final. The last time I was free on Cup Final day was in 1949-50, when Liverpool played Arsenal at Wembley. If ever there was a golden opportunity to see the match this was it. But the game was to be televised, and apart from the cost of the trip (to a struggling young hardware salesman, cum part-time entertainer) the lure of this (then) novelty was too strong. I stayed home and watched my heroes on telly—and they lost 2—0.

There were not many gags cracked in the Dodd household *that* afternoon.

But I did see Liverpool's home game against Arsenal in April last year. It resulted in revenge for that Cup Final beating. Not only did the Reds from Anfield lick the Reds from Highbury 5—0, but the result clinched the League Championship. A great day for Bill Shankly and his boys —and for Doddy and the other roaring Kop-ites.

It was tattyphilarious!

Although my shouts are usually for Liverpool, I wouldn't like anyone to think that I don't admire Everton, who also help to make Merseyside the most exciting Soccer centre.

When the two clash no quarter is asked or given. But there is still a friendly rivalry between the clubs. And that can do nothing but good for the cause of the greatest game in the world.

If I were asked to pick a team from Liverpool and Everton, I'm sure that this one would take a lot of beating: Lawrence; Lawler, Byrne; Milne, Yeats, Stevenson; Callaghan, Hunt, St. John, Smith, Thompson.

I still manage to turn-out for the odd game (and they are very odd!) for the Showbiz team, and it is generally agreed that I am their best inside-right since Old Mother Riley.

Travelling around the country on my firewood-round I don't get the chance to see many matches. So I keep in touch, thanks to Charles Buchan's "Football Monthly". I buy it every week!

Tatty-Bye everybody!

GLOSSARY.

Tatty-Bye—Goodbye.
Tattyphilarious—Marvellous.
Plumptiousness—Dignified Delight.
Gertitude—Sentiment.

TAKE a team like Liverpool, a crowd like the Kop and a manager whose name crops up whenever fanaticism is discussed. Set down their story according to St. John and you've got all the ingredients of a brash, bouncing best-seller.

So what went wrong when Ian St. John mixed the magic ingredients?

For the Anfield Scot—currently running third behind Ringo and Ken Dodd on the list of Merseyside idols—has written one of those autobiographies ("Boom at the Kop"—Pelham Books, 21s.) that every Soccer star seems to find it his duty to attempt.

The formula is that which has drearily served a hundred or so of St. John's predecessors.

His father died after taking him to a match

Childhood memories; the first club; the break into the Big Leagues; great games I have played; great players I have known; my World Team.

St. John follows a well-worn track.

And the pity of this stereotype saga is that the excitement, the humour, the tragedy of what has been an enthralling clogs-to-caviar career only rarely breaks through.

At the age of six, St. John was taken by his father to Motherwell's ground, just forty yards from his home.

He recalls: "It was a bitterly cold Saturday afternoon. The rain swept down in torrents and we got thoroughly soaked. My father went down with pleurisy the same night. It turned to pneumonia and he died a few days later."

This tragic introduction to the game didn't stop St. John joining the huge ranks of Scotland's Soccer-mad youngsters.

He progressed through schools and Boys Clubs football, joined a potentially prodigiously talented Motherwell side with whom he won his first Scottish cap, became involved in the inevitable money wrangle and in 1961 he teamed up with Liverpool—and Bill Shankly.

This fierce, intense managerial maestro whose dedication has had so much to do with the Liverpool success story is paid due tribute by St. John.

One day, somebody is going to collect and publish all the Shankly anecdotes which buzz around the British football scene. St. John contributes two to the prospective collection.

He takes us into the Liverpool coach as it nudges its way through the Wembley-bound crowds on Cup Final Day, 1965.

"The radio was playing all the way to the stadium and one of the programmes was a recorded edition of 'Desert Island Discs'. You can imagine the roar that went up when the announcer said: '*And our castaway this week is . . . Mr. Bill Shankly*'.

"The boss's choice of records was pretty hilarious too . . . 'You'll Never Walk Alone,' 'When the Saints Go Marching In,' in fact, all the songs the Kop Choir sings. *What a man! He eats, drinks, sleeps and even sings Liverpool Football Club.*"

St. John's account of Shankly's pre-Final dressing room speech is also worth recording.

"You are going out there to win because you are the best team. Leeds are honoured, and lucky, to be on the same field as you. You must not disappoint the finest spectators any club has in the world . . . there can only be one result."

IAN ST. JOHN

TRAGEDY!

That was the start of the Soccer life of IAN ST. JOHN

But only when he discusses the choristers of the Kop and their high priest, Bill Shankly, does St. John's tale lift itself out of the familiar autobiographical rut. Apart from one frank chapter devoted to the men who

pick Scotland's international side.

Laying his head on the international chopping block, St. John declares: "*I couldn't care less if I am never picked to play for Scotland again.*"

The reason centres around last year's England-Scotland clash at Wembley when the Scots, boosted as the greatest side ever to pull on the deep blue jerseys, escaped with a providential draw against a nine-man England team.

St. John slams the Scottish tactics, dismisses former team-manager Ian McColl as a man: "without that all-important know-how," and claims he was made a scapegoat when—a few days after scoring the equaliser against England—he was dropped from Scotland's World Cup squad.

He concludes: "My bread and butter is at Liverpool. There I get a wonderful deal. There, I know my football is appreciated."

All in all, it's a story which, with just a few names and facts altered, could have been written by almost any of St. John's contemporaries.

But he's fortunate to be able to finish his narrative with this story:

It concerns a small mission hall just outside Anfield which frequently displays religious slogans.

One day, a slogan posed the question: "What would you do if Jesus came back?"

Says the author: "Beneath it someone, from the Kop I feel sure, had scrawled the words: "*Move St. John to inside-right.*"

BILL SHANKLY
A dedicated maestro

By JOHN ANTHONY

FAITH and PRIDE

LEN PARKER

ONE of the greatest mistakes anyone can make in Soccer is to suggest to Bill Shankly that Liverpool at any time are not doing well. I made that mistake once.

It was just after Liverpool had rejoined the First Division. Shankly's defence of his team was complete. At such times the gravel voice becomes thicker, the Scottish accent broader. It is not always easy to understand ALL the words — it is impossible not to understand the FULL meaning.

Shankly's faith in his team cannot be shaken. That, perhaps as much as the undoubted ability of that team, has brought Liverpool almost unequalled success over the past three years.

They have won one League title and are well on the way to a second. They have won the F.A. Cup. They have become one of Europe's most-powerful and most-feared teams.

Shankly is volatile, explosive and full of pride. He demands extreme effort from his players in training as well as on match days. He gets it and he deserves it.

Of course, Liverpool are not perfect; of course, Shankly knows it, and his players know it. But faith, they say, can move mountains — and Shankly proclaims his faith in Liverpool with a fervour which MUST inspire his players.

He once said: "There's only one way to do anything in football — that's flat-out. I want a man who will go through a brick wall with a broken leg . . . and still come out the other side shooting for goal. If he can do that, he is good enough to play for Liverpool!"

I have no doubt he would have set similar standards and shown the same pride had he still been at Carlisle, Grimsby, Huddersfield or Workington, where he has also managed footballers.

Undoubtedly, Shankly is a football fanatic. As a player he asked and gave no quarter. He won caps for Scotland and appeared in two F.A. Cup finals with Preston.

The measure of his fanaticism may be judged by the fact that when Liverpool played West Ham in the 1964 Charity Shield, Shankly went among his beloved Kop fans and talked with them. Not a man there could boast greater pride in the Anfield club.

Like fellow-Scot Matt Busby — equally Soccer-wise but so different in approach — Shankly left the pits for football. After 16 League games with Carlisle, he was sought by Preston — and turned them down.

After his brother, Sandy, exploded: "You're daft, man!" Shankly changed his mind, caught up with the Preston representative as the train was moving out of the station and signed, *en route* for Newcastle. The fee: £500. Shankly

was 18 and happy at Carlisle — but he stayed 16 years with Preston.

It was characteristic when, on the eve of an international against England, he had to pull out — because it was found he had been playing for months with a badly displaced cartilage.

"If there is anything I demand in a footballer, it is courage and toughness," he has said. No-one can accuse him of lacking either quality.

As a manager, he showed courage when he bought big for Liverpool — Ron Yeats, Gordon Milne, Willie Stevenson, Ian St. John, Peter Thompson, Geoff Strong, Phil Chisnall and John Ogston.

The last three have not been able to hold regular first-team places — but

Strong has been rated the best stand-in in First Division football. And at Wembley last year, he amply repaid the £40,000 fee Liverpool gave Arsenal for him.

Whenever I see Shankly, I think of the story which stems from a Blackpool victory at Anfield. It was a shock. One fan, imitating Shankly's Scottish burr, observed: "The Fitba' League will never-r-r accept this result!"

I do not think Shankly would have gone that far, because he is a realist, and knows you cannot win them all.

Today, Shankly is leading his red-shirted warriors towards new conquests. And I will bet he is already plotting how to get his hands on the European Cup next season!

. . . HOW SHANKLY TOOK LIVERPOOL TO THE TOP

▲ April 1966

CHARLES BUCHAN'S
FOOTBALL
MONTHLY

JUNE, 1966

2/6

WORLD CHAMPIONSHIP · JULES RIMET CUP · ENGLAND · 1966

CUP FINAL
SPECIAL

CHARLES BUCHAN'S
FOOTBALL
MONTHLY

FOUNDED IN 1951
BY CHARLES BUCHAN
CAPTAIN OF SUNDERLAND
ARSENAL AND ENGLAND

JULY, 1966   **No. 179**

EDITED BY
JOHN THOMPSON
JOE SARL

ASSISTANT EDITORS
PAT COLLINS
MALCOLM CUMMING

CONTENTS

COLOUR PICTURES:
     PETER STUART

ADVERTISEMENT MANAGER:
     G. A. IRELAND

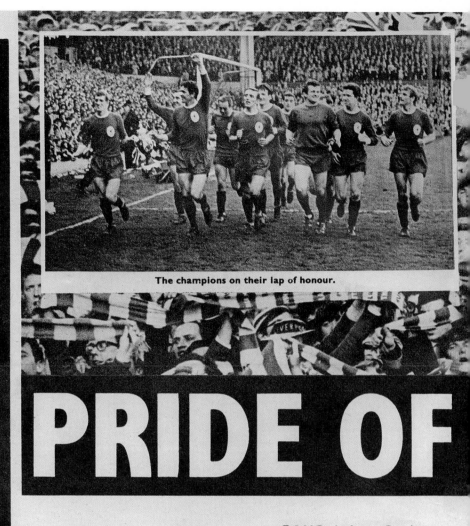

The champions on their lap of honour.

PRIDE OF

They said they were great ... they've proved it says PAT COLLINS

LONG before Cassius Clay said it about himself they were saying it on Merseyside. About themselves. "WE ARE THE GREATEST IN THE WORLD." Liverpool and Everton fans said it about their teams. The players about their supporters. With equal conviction.

From Anfield Park, Liverpool manager Bill Shankly spoke for BOTH clubs when he repeated the claim, and added: "They deserve only the best teams and the best football."

With the Football League Championship and the F.A. Cup lodged in their city none could dispute that they have got just that.

They sing, they shout, they sway. Their songs of praise (for the Reds and the Blues) and derision (for their rivals, or unfortunate referees) are blatantly stolen and re-phrased by less inventive, and harmonious fans elsewhere.

Nowhere are there fans to match their spontaneity, their wit or the sharp edge of their sarcasm in song. Nobody is spared or overlooked. No name or situation stumps them. Into wide-eyed European cities they have carried

▲ July 1966

MERSEYSIDE!

their songs and those huge banners to the indulgent and the incredulous.

Prime Minister Harold Wilson himself heard a rousing reveille on Cup Final morn. Said the P.M: "I heard the noise outside (No. 10). They were singing "ee-aye-addio, Harold's still in bed." Only their timing was out—he was up.

Liverpool, England's most successful Soccer city, is also our most melodious.

Without any respect for feelings in West Bromwich they will tell you that there is only one reason why they didn't make a clean sweep of the honours by adding the Football League Cup to the city's bag. Well, two!

Neither Everton or Liverpool took part in it. It is as simple as that, they say.

While they were still congratulating him in the dressing-room on being the Cup-winning captain, Brian Labone told me: "As we came down the Empire Way to the Stadium for the Final I could see nothing but our supporters. I could have cried at the way they cheered us every yard of the way.

"They were still cheering us on when Wednesday's second goal put us two down and apparently out of the reckoning. How could you let down fans like that?"

Those Goodison supporters, and their brethren from across the way at Anfield, have been given reason enough to celebrate by their heroes. Their last five seasons of plenty amount to this fantastic record . . .

1961-2	Second Division champions	Liverpool
1962-3	League champions	Everton
1963-4	League champions (with Everton five points behind, third)	Liverpool
1964-5	F.A. Cup winners	Liverpool
1965-6	F.A. Cup winners	Everton
1965-6	League champions	Liverpool

Then there are Liverpool's last two sallies into European competition . . .

1964-5 European Cup semi-finalists
1965-6 European Cup-Winners' Cup finalists

It would seem that Merseyside's fanatical fans are getting what they deserve . . . the best.

Now their teams head England's challenge in Europe next season. Somewhere, sometime the colourful, cheerful, aggressive "Liverpool sound" will be heard with redoubled volume.

Whatever reaction it arouses be sure that it will demand respect for the men who inspire it.

Liverpool's second goal against Chelsea which clinched the League title.

SUCCESS

by
TOMMY
SMITH
Liverpool

has come our way and I am proud to have taken part in it

I WAS born in the famous Scotland Road district—so who else would I wish to play for but Liverpool? But it was really due to my father's unfortunate passing-on when I was only 15, that prompted me to become a professional footballer.

I first went to St. John's School in North Dingle Road and played at full-back for the school team. I then won a scholarship to the Cardinal Godfrey College where I still played Soccer—but at centre-half.

But I never thought of the game as a means of livelihood, for I had set my mind on becoming an architect and was studying when the blow fell on the family.

I was offered ground-staff terms at the time we lost my father and it was purely the opportunity to be able to contribute to the family budget, that made me burn my boats and accept.

I've never regretted the decision, for if I ever had any qualms about my ability to succeed in Soccer they were dispelled in my first season when—though still only 15—I was chosen five times for the reserve team. Not bad for a virtual schoolboy!

Mind you, most of my games were with the "C" and "A" teams. By then I had been converted to centre-forward, and later again to inside-left.

The following season this became my regular position and at 17 I made my first-team debut. Gordon Milne was unable to play due to an injury and I was picked to play right-half. The game was against Birmingham and we won 5-1. I was cock-a-hoop!

Naturally, Gordon was back for the next game but I had enjoyed my taste of the big-time, and at 18 I was a member of the England Youth team that won the Junior World Cup (so-called) in which we played five games without having a single goal scored against us. We scored 15.

It was a great team, and included players like Badger and Bernard Shaw, of Sheffield United, Ron Harris, of Chelsea, and Sissons of West Ham.

But at Liverpool I was still a reserve player until early last season when, with Ian St. John injured, I again stepped into the first eleven, at inside-left. After half-a-dozen games it was back to the reserves for me—until the European Cup game against Anderlecht.

I was given the No. 10 shirt, with instructions to drop back to wing-half to allow Gordon Milne to move up into the attack. It seemed to work.

And, luckily for me, that's the way it

has been ever since for although I still wear the No. 10 shirt, I play more or less a normal half-back role.

I am usually in the forward line for the kick-off but only for that. And neither the boss nor I would want to change that number—it has been such a successful omen.

Very successful from my point of view, for since that Anderlecht game I have never lost my place, and it has been a great thrill going through to the semifinal of last year's European Cup, and, of course, winning the F.A. Cup at Wembley in May 1965.

We're back in Europe

This was *my* biggest day so far.

It is an honour which reflects on the club as a whole, not on individual players. And I feel very much the same about our winning the League Championship—for this, too, is very much a team success and again guarantees our entry into next season's European Cup.

We were, of course, bitterly disappointed that we failed to win the European Cup-Winners' Cup at Hampden Park. We were not cocky—but felt confident that we had the ability to beat Borussia Dortmund, and as we went into extra time, we were sure we would do it.

It felt like the end of the world when they scored their freak, winning goal!

But I have a sneaking feeling of personal pride every time I recall one particular goal I have scored. It was last season, on our own ground at Anfield, against our traditional "enemy" from across the Park—Everton!

I was playing full-back that day, standing-in for Chris Lawler who was

injured, and we licked them 5-0! My goal was a simple affair. I had moved-up with our attack when the ball came across from the wing. I headed it—and there it was nestling safely in the net.

Generally speaking, my job is two-fold —to stop the opposition, and to help keep our forwards ticking over. We've done that pretty successfully this past season, and I only wish that my late dad had been able to watch the part I have played in our favourite team's success.

"Stick at your French, son—we meet them on July 20."

WHEN THE MAGIC TOUCH FAILED!

This was the second when Liverpool's hopes of the "double" of Football League title and European Cup-Winners' Cup ended. Ron Yeats lies helpless in the net at Hampden Park as Borussia Dortmund score the winner in the Final.

IF
YOU
ARE
A
SCOUSE

... then you will treasure these pictures. They show the world's three top trophies on display in one English city—Liverpool, at Goodison Park where Liverpool won the F.A. Charity Shield against Everton. Right, Roger Hunt (Liverpool) and Ray Wilson (Everton) parade with the World Cup they helped England to win. Below, Ron Yeats (Liverpool) with the Football League Cup, and Brian Labone (Everton) and F.A. Cup.

▲ October 1966

CHARLES BUCHAN'S

FOOTBALL
MONTHLY

WORLD'S
GREATEST
SOCCER
MAGAZINE

NOVEMBER,
1966

2/6

INSIDE
GIANT COLOUR
PICTURE
OF EVERTON

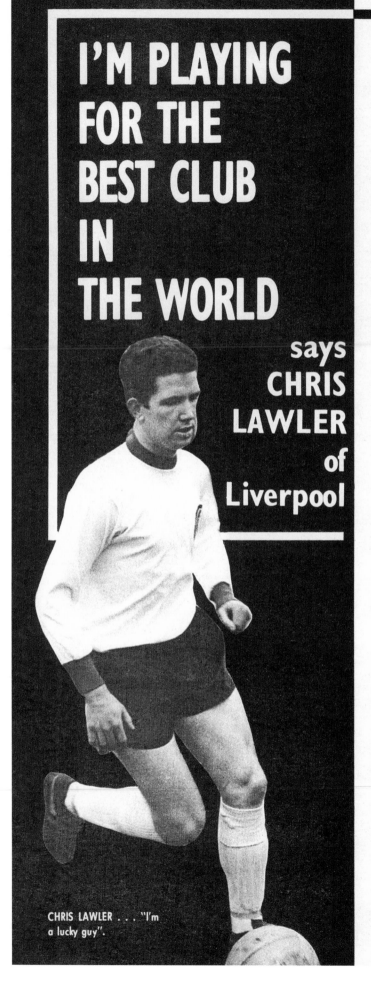

I'M PLAYING FOR THE BEST CLUB IN THE WORLD

says CHRIS LAWLER of Liverpool

CHRIS LAWLER . . . "I'm a lucky guy".

I'M a lucky guy! Though my career so far consists of only two seasons of First Division football I can already look back on achievements that many outstanding players have not realised after a life-time in the game — a Cup winners' medal, a League Championship medal, and appearances in the European Cup Winners' Cup Final and the European Cup semi-final.

And in addition I am playing for the best club (and team) in the world thus realising an ambition that I have cherished since I was a schoolboy.

Like so many Merseysiders, as a kid I was Soccer-daft. Liverpool were my club and my individual idol was the legendary Billy Liddell, a great player and an off-the-field example to anyone in any walk of life.

And I can't remember the day when I didn't want to follow the famous Scot and play for Liverpool.

I was born in Norris Green and attended St. Teresa's School where I played centre-half. And it was in this position that I played for Liverpool Boys and England Boys.

I didn't know it at the time, but I was being carefully watched by Liverpool's local scout, the late Thomas 'Tosh' Moore, and when I left school at 15 I was asked if I would like to join the Anfield ground staff.

Would I like? Wild horses wouldn't have stopped me, and so began the usual climb through the junior and 'A' teams still as a centre-half playing the odd game at full-back if required.

In fact I made my debut in the League side as pivot in a game with West Bromwich Albion at Anfield, which was drawn 2-2.

I gained my first representative honour as centre-half for England Youth against Switzerland at Leyton Orient's ground and towards the end of the 1963-64 season again played for the League side over Easter, when Ron Yeats was under suspension.

By this time I had played a number of games in the reserves as a stop-gap full-back and early in the season before last came my big chance when I was chosen at right-back with Gerry Byrne on the other flank.

I must have pleased the boss, for I managed to retain the position and before the season ended I had played in seven European Cup-ties, and had gone through the F.A. Cup series, ending with our victory over Leeds at Wembley. That is a day stamped on my memory. It

▲ Gift Book 1966–67

CELEBRATION for a team . . . Liverpool win the 1964 League title. On the right Lawler, then not a regular first-teamer.

was a wonderful feeling — we all felt so very proud.

But my European Cup baptism is another game that I will never forget. I hadn't been playing regularly with the first team for very long when we were drawn against Anderlecht, the first leg to be played at Anfield. We won 3-0 and won the second leg 1-0 in Brussels.

Then came the marathon three-game stint against Cologne (no-score twice, 2-2 at the third meeting). That resulted in Liverpool reaching the semi-final by virtue of winning the toss.

We had already won the F.A. Cup at Wembley the previous Saturday, when on Tuesday, May 4 we beat the famous Inter-Milan 3-1 at Anfield in the first leg — and we had visions of a double crown. But it was not to be for the following week in Milan, we lost the second leg 3-0!

But the 'Reds' again enjoyed a successful season last term and I personally have had another couple of red letter days — my two appearances for the England Under-23 side, at Norwich against France, and at Southampton against Yugoslavia.

I'm keeping my fingers crossed for a full England cap, and if it could possibly arrive in this new season then so much the better.

But I'm not building-up any hopes on this I don't want to disappoint myself too much if it doesn't happen.

And if it doesn't? Well — I've still a lot to be thankful for. If my future is as bright as my brief past has been I shall not have much to complain about.

After all — I'm playing for the best club in the world . . .

CELEBRATION for two . . . Lawler and Geraldine Brown celebrate Liverpool's 1965 Cup win two days before their wedding.

CHARLES BUCHAN'S
FOOTBALL
MONTHLY

SEPTEMBER, 1967

PETER THOMPSON
Liverpool

Bill Shankly . . . "let me get at 'em"   Tony Hateley . . . he should fit in

Power build-up at
ANFIELD!

THERE has been an atmosphere of seething expectancy at Anfield this summer while Liverpool generate fresh power for another assault on the First Division, the F.A. Cup and anything else they take a fancy to.

This is hardly surprising since last season the much vaunted Reds won nothing, following on five years of sweet success. Koppites will hardly rate a single season of failure as complete disaster but they must be thrown at least one major honour this winter to adjust the balance.

Equally determined that they shall have it is manager Bill Shankly who has spent the close season in a state of restrained explosion.

His "let me get at 'em" attitude as he surveys the opposition promises a campaign of high drama in the north west where Everton and Manchester United, the champions, loom large as the immediate giants for slaying.

Shankly must also fend off challenges from other quarters — Leeds, Spurs, Nottingham Forest, Chelsea—if he intends to get back the championship. The Liverpool manager has not been content just to fume. He charged in to grab Tony Hateley when Chelsea's

PETER MORRIS predicts another Liverpool challenge

manager, Tommy Docherty, decided to recoup some of the £100,000 spent on yet another Stamford Bridge misfit.

Once, Shankly had the option on Hateley during his Villa days but he had to waive it. Now it has cost him £90,000 to get the big fellow to Anfield.

Shankly will not feel he has been "done" if Hateley does what Shankly thinks he will—get his head to those many tempting centres floated across by wingers Ian Callaghan and Peter Thompson. It is fair to assume that Hateley will fit in more easily with Liverpool's front line than ever he did at Stamford Bridge.

It now looks as though Ian St John will in future operate as a deep-lying inside man, leaving Hateley and Roger Hunt as the twin spearheads.

Of course, much of the money

Shankly spent on Hateley he already had in reserve from the sale for £32,000, this summer, of his former England wing-half, Gordon Milne, to down-on-their-luck Blackpool.

The Hateley signing by no means ends the reinforcing process at Anfield where they have cash in plenty to show when the right player becomes available. Liverpool's chairman, Mr Sidney Reakes, has stated publicly that his club wants to see a star name or two added to the strength—and quickly.

In addition, there have been several less publicised captures to bolster up Liverpool's reserve strength — which promises to be a formidable safeguard against injuries.

For instance, Scunthorpe's highly-promising young goalkeeper, Ray Clemence, was signed for £18,000; David Wilson, Preston's skilful little winger, was another purchase — and remember, not all that long ago, Wilson was almost on the fringe of the England team.

Fullback Emlyn Hughes, signed for an almost unprecedented fee—for an unknown—of £65,000 from Blackpool, is now firmly established in the League side but not so clear is the future of some of manager Shankly's earlier buys.

He paid £30,000 last season for Wrexham's teen-age full-back pair, Tommy Wall and Stewart Mason, and so far has kept them both in the reserves. In fact, at the end of the season, both were in the third team.

And Shankly has not yet been able to fit in former Aberdeen goalkeeper, John Ogston, or Phil Chisnall, the one-time Manchester schools star, signed from Manchester United.

There must be a query, too, against the name of Geoff Strong. Will he be used as a wing-half—as he was towards the end of last season—or as a forward? Much will depend on whether or not veteran Willie Stevenson leaves Anfield.

If their spending spree goes on, then Liverpool may be able to afford to let Stevenson go as well as Chisnall and Alf Arrowsmith, a useful forward, who looked at one time worthy of a first team place.

Liverpool's playing decline—if you can really call it that—came after their European Cup defeat by Ajax of Amsterdam. Until then they had always been among the pace setters—and, at times, still looked the most accomplished team in the First Division.

After the bitter disappointment of that Ajax defeat, Liverpool never quite got back into the groove. In the end they had to be satisfied with fifth place with three more points than Everton who finished with a menacing flourish.

It was Everton, of course, who ended Liverpool's F.A. Cup run in that high tension clash at Goodison. That was the last chance of honours gone for the Reds in season 1966-67.

Certainly, at the start of the campaign, it would have been hard to see Liverpool not winning *something*.

But that was the way of it and now the faithful of the Kop have forgotten the past and look with covetous eyes on the future—the immediate future.

LIVERPOOL Standing — Byrne, Strong, Clemence
Arrowsmith

rence, Lawler, Stevenson, Hunt. Sitting—St. John, Callaghan,
eley, Yeats, Hughes, Thompson, Smith.

IAN ST. JOHN

OF LIVERPOOL

The Scot who became a scouse

THEY can have their Tony Hateleys, their Wyn and Ron Davieses, their John Ritchies, but for one famous manager I know, the best centre-forward of them all is Liverpool's Ian St. John. And that manager ISN'T Bill Shankly!

When you consider that St. John has been with Liverpool now for almost six years, and been a consistent member of the first team ever since he arrived, you begin to realise just how great a part this Scot from Motherwell has played in the Anfield club's long run of success.

Today, when people talk about the great centre-forwards in the game, the names of players like the two Davieses, Hateley and Ritchie trip off their tongues . . . *seldom do I hear St. John's name.* And yet . . . put him in the open transfer market, and what would his price be?

It's incredible to think that when he was signed in May, 1961, he was Liverpool's record-priced buy—at £35,000. Bill Shankly's, too.

How much value has he given Liverpool since that May day? In terms of service and games alone — plenty.

It is significant that in every season since St. John has been at Anfield, Liverpool have achieved something . . . promotion, an F.A. Cup semifinal, the League title, the F.A. Cup, the League title, European Soccer.

Of course, as Bill Shankly would hasten to point out about his beloved Liverpool, one player doesn't make a team. I can just imagine Bill growling: "We've got ELEVEN of 'em here at Liverr-r-pool!" But, pound for pound, physically and financially speaking, I don't think

IAN ST. JOHN

any player has given greater value than St. John.

I remember reading about him when he turned out at inside-right for Motherwell. He was 19. And the writer said: "He was a centre-forward — now he is trying hard to establish himself as Motherwell's regular inside-right."

By the start of 1959, he was a centre-forward again — and out of action with a wrist injury. As the years went by, he had more than his fair share of trouble . . . a cartilage operation in 1960, an operation for appendicitis in 1964 which saw him miss the start of the season . . . and, earlier that year, a hat-trick in a 6-1 thrashing of Sheffield United which revealed the secret of a year-old injury.

Bill Shankly said at the time: "No-one, apart from those close to him at Anfield, realised just what he had been up against. The condition —

severe pain from an old ankle injury — was constantly aggravated over 12 months . . . he was constantly under treatment, but he gritted his teeth and never complained.''

That hat-trick day was the first time in a year he had gone through a game without feeling the rough edge of pain from that old injury.

St. John is the player of whom Charlie Mitten, then manager of Newcastle said: ''He is the nearest approach I have seen to Di Stefano.'' St. John was 20 then; about to lead Scotland against the Irish in one of his early international outings.

There was transfer talk in the air, talk of what it would cost . . . around £20,000. Then along came Mitten and Newcastle to offer £25,000 — which was turned down flat.

By March, 1960, Blackburn were reported to be ready to go to £30,000, but it was May, 1961, when he left his home-town club for Liverpool.

And Newcastle were the rivals pipped in the race.

Bill Shankly went north to watch Motherwell play Hamilton Acas.: correction — to watch St. John play against Hamilton Acas. He had been tipped off, this Scot who managed Liverpool, that St. John could be got at a price.

By half-time, Shankly had seen enough of the game and St. John. When the players came out for the second half, Bill was still in the boardroom, negotiating for the transfer of St. John. Midnight came, and the deal was sealed with a handshake. Newcastle were also on the scene, but they had left their arrival too late.

Ian St. John made his debut for Liverpool in a Liverpool Senior Cup Final against Everton. Soon he was being described as ''the hidden force in no-man's land between the mid-line and the four front chasers''. Shankly's verdict: ''He sees situations others don't see.''

I like the story Alan Ball, now with Everton, tells when he made *his* debut for Blackpool at Anfield.

Ball and St. John had a bit of a brush, whereupon a wag from the Kop shouted to Ball: *''Watch it, Wack or you'll get his halo wrapped round your neck!''*

IT'S A STORY WHICH SUMS UP HOW A SCOT FROM MOTHERWELL BECAME A SCOUSE BY ADOPTION...AND WAS READILY ACCEPTED AS SUCH BY THOSE WHO LOOK AT SOCCER THROUGH RED-COLOURED EYEBALLS.

JERRY DAWSON

Star Strip

PETER THOMPSON
LIVERPOOL

PETER THOMPSON CAME INTO THE PRESTON NORTH END SIDE AT THE AGE OF 17, SHORTLY AFTER TOMMY FINNEY RETIRED, AND WAS IMMEDIATELY HAILED AS HIS SUCCESSOR.

CRIKEY! THERE'LL NEVER BE ANOTHER FINNEY, BUT THIS LAD WILL DO TO BE GOING ON WITH...

IN 1962 THOMPSON, STILL A RAW YOUTH, SHOT THE ONLY GOAL OF A MARATHON FIFTH ROUND CUP-TIE — AGAINST LIVERPOOL! TWICE PRESTON HAD HELD BILL SHANKLY'S MEN TO GOALLESS DRAWS, AND THE TEAMS PLAYED FIVE HOURS BEFORE THE GOAL WAS SCORED.

DURING HIS EARLY YEARS THOMPSON PROVED JUST AS VERSATILE AS FINNEY, OPERATING ON EITHER WING OR AT CENTRE-FORWARD WITH EQUAL EFFECTIVENESS. HE CARRIES ONE OF THE HARDEST SHOTS IN THE GAME, AND SOME THINK HE WOULD STILL BE MOST DANGEROUS LEADING THE ATTACK. HE DOESN'T SCORE VERY OFTEN, BUT WILL NOW AND THEN PULL SOMETHING OFF FOR THE BIG OCCASION.

BILL SHANKLY RECALLS: OVER A YEAR PASSED BEFORE I BOUGHT PETER FROM NORTH END, AFTER I WAS UNABLE TO PERSUADE HUDDERSFIELD TO PART WITH O'GRADY. A BARGAIN AT £40,000, THOMPSON WOULD FETCH OVER TWICE THAT FIGURE TODAY.

OF COURSE, HE IS ONE OF SHANKLY'S BEST BUYS. HIS MIRACULOUS BALL CONTROL QUICKLY MADE HIM A KOP FAVOURITE, AND IN HIS FIRST SEASON AT ANFIELD, 1963-4, HE CREATED MANY OPENINGS FOR ST. JOHN AND HUNT AS 'POOL RACED TO THE TOP OF THE LEAGUE.

BOB BOND

GOAL!

HE HAMMERED IN TWO MAGNIFICENT GOALS IN THE TITLE-CLINCHING 5-0 WIN OVER ARSENAL IN 1964.

ONE OF HIS BEST WAS IN THE 1965 F.A. CUP SEMI-FINAL AGAINST CHELSEA, WHEN HE BURST THROUGH TO BEAT BONETTI WITH A ROCKET SHOT — THE FIRST, VITAL GOAL IN A 2-0 WIN.

ALREADY AN ENGLAND CAP, HE PLAYED AGAINST SCOTLAND AT WEMBLEY THAT YEAR (AT OUTSIDE-RIGHT), AND SOON AFTER RETURNED TO PLAY A PROMINENT PART IN 'POOL'S CUP FINAL WIN. ON HIS BEST DAYS HE TOUCHES THE VERY HEIGHTS WITH HIS SCINTILLATING DRIBBLING, SKATING PAST A FULL-BACK AS IF HE JUST ISN'T THERE.

THOMPSON IS SLIGHTLY INCONSISTENT, HOWEVER, AND THIS HAS COST HIM A REGULAR INTERNATIONAL PLACE SO FAR. COULD HE BE AT HIS PEAK WHEN THE TIME COMES FOR ENGLAND TO DEFEND THE WORLD CUP IN 1970?

▲ April 1968 | May 1968 ▶

TOMMY SMITH
Liverpool

The Anfield local boy who has become the game's most formidable "sweeper", an expert penalty-taker and an England Under-23 star.

EVERTON OR LIVERPOOL?

CILLA BLACK admits now to being (whisper it) a Reds fan

D O I like football? Of course I do—you have to if you are a Liverpudlian, and especially where I lived. But I never quite knew which of the city's two teams to support.

Most families are whole-hearted supporters of one or the other—but we had to be different.

Me dad and me eldest brother George were raving Everton fans—and still are. So as a child I followed their lead. But the next in line, our John and our Alan, plumped for Liverpool at an early age.

Which left me stuck right in the middle of four men—but my problem was solved when Bobby Willis (now my fiancé) first joined me as road manager.

Bobby is a true Red-eye—a Liverpool supporter straight down the line. What else could poor little me do except "join the club?"

But the funny thing is that I have never seen Liverpool play at home. I've watched them away from home when I have been on tour—and I've yet to see them win a game. Always they seem to draw, consequently I'm not terribly popular around Anfield way—or with me two young brothers! But it's O.K. with me dad and our George!

As a matter of fact—whenever I go to a football match, the team I'm supporting always seem to lose. When I was in Glasgow a few months ago, I went to Ibrox Park to watch Rangers—and they lost for the first time that season.

But losers or not, I thoroughly enjoyed watching one of their players. Wee Willie something-or-other (Johnston?) they called him—he was smashing.

I like football chiefly because I can understand the game—it isn't as complicated as some sports. Cricket bores me—but I like football even on the television. And if anything can entertain *me* on television, it must be good.

But I do enjoy the atmosphere at the game —and I can get as excited as anyone.

TONY HATELEY
(Liverpool) out-jumps
ENGLAND (Spurs)

How lucky can a 21-year-old guy be?

asks EMLYN HUGHES, of Liverpool

HOW lucky can a guy be? Here I am—a 21-year-old—and a regular first-teamer with one of the top clubs in the great, great, Soccer-mad city of Liverpool.

When I look back to my early days and remember how close I came to packing the game in—I go cold! This was when I was with Blackpool whom I joined from a junior club, Roose F.C., in my home town of Barrow.

I was playing regularly enough for the " A " or " B " team every Saturday but working in a garage in Barrow and training on my own at nights.

When I first went to Blackpool for trials I wasn't very strong, and was sent home for a year and given a special diet designed to build-up my physique. When I returned I was taken on the part-time staff and although I never heard any complaints from the then manager, Mr. Ronnie Suart, I began to feel that I would never make it . . .

. . . until an amazing chain of luck started—slowly at first, becoming almost a whirlwind. Originally an inside-forward, I was playing wing-half for the Blackpool junior sides when for one " A " team match a full-back failed to turn-up. I was given his place, and kept it for

▲ Gift Book 1968–69

NO PLACE FOR NEUTRALS

several games, before being promoted to the reserves.

Next—Jimmy Armfield was called-up for England duty, Tommy Thompson moved over to take his position and I was given the left-back spot. This was at the end of season 1965–66, and in the following term I became first choice in this position.

I learned a lot playing alongside Jimmy Armfield but even so I was the most surprised (and delighted) player in the game when before that season was over I found myself at Anfield Road.

What a difference! I like Blackpool, so much so, that I would dearly love to settle there when I finish playing. I owe a lot to the club, too —for had I not been given my chance there, I could well be back in the garage business in Barrow.

But Liverpool—as a city and as a football club is a different world. First of all there is the difference in crowds—40,000 to 60,000 spectators against the 14,000 or so at Bloomfield Road. The famous Kop, alone, regularly contains more than that figure.

Then again, in Blackpool one could walk the streets and pleasure palaces, unnoticed and unknown. Not so on Merseyside where every male—man and boy—and lots of females just live for Soccer. You support *either* Liverpool or Everton —you daren't support both—and no-one seems disinterested in the game.

The supporters recognise you wherever you go and have no inhibitions about speaking to you. And the one topic immediately a game is over is—the next match.

The city is alive with Soccer atmosphere and if one is to survive in this neck of the woods, one has no option—or desire—to be anything but dedicated. And the whole set-up at Anfield is designed to this one end.

Training—as one would expect under such a football fanatical boss as Mr. Bill Shankly—is hard and tough. But very little of it is done without the ball. We are training to be the best football players in the land—and we are given a ball to play with.

Everything is so utterly professional and success is a *must*! To

lose is a sin—to be avoided at all costs.

And look at the perks! Since joining Liverpool, I have played three times for the England Under-23 team (against Wales, Italy, and against Scotland at Hampden Park), have travelled to Germany, Spain and Sweden to play Soccer and have enjoyed two holidays in Majorca at the club's expense.

And I have a good salary and my own car. Not being married, I am in digs not far from the Anfield ground with team-mate Alun Evans, where it is a case of *"first up—best dressed"*. Yes—even just living is fun.

I enjoy every minute of the game although last season I was not in my favourite full-back position. My job with Liverpool (so far) has been in midfield alongside Ian St. John, with Ian Callaghan falling back to help out in away games. I have played full-back only when injuries to colleagues have made it necessary, but I hope eventually to move to the back line.

Although in midfield one is much more in the thick of the game (nowadays most of the play seems to be in midfield) I prefer the full-back position, chiefly, I suppose, because the game is always coming to you. But wherever you play in a Liverpool side, you are very much part of a *team*.

Particularly in defence! If I pick up a ball in the danger area, I never have to look for a colleague, nor do I have to start running. Immediately, a couple of the lads will be calling for the ball—one coming alongside from behind to take a square pass—one from up front, either coming to take a forward pass, or moving into a space to take it!

And, of course, the improvement in my play is very noticeable for not only is one playing *for* a good side, but also playing against one. Due to the club's success in this decade, *everyone* is out to beat Liverpool. And we are there to see that they don't!

ALUN EVANS (above) . . . **even just living with him is fun.**

IAN ST. JOHN (right) . . . **my job is to link up in mid-field with him.**

Gordon Hodgson, former Liverpool goalscoring record holder, and (right) Roger Hunt, who broke it.

IT'S HARD TO SCORE THESE DAYS

THE six-week drag . . . that's what I called that anxious pressure spell last season when I was trying to get the goal which would set a new League scoring record for Liverpool, my only club.

That great Anfield servant, the late Gordon Hodgson, had established the previous record with 233 League goals in pre-war days and, obviously, I was keen to try and beat it.

But last winter proved to be just about my leanest scoring season since I made my League debut for the Reds in September, 1959.

I just couldn't put the ball into the net as I used to and when I did get the kind of chances I thrive on I muffed them. In fact, the comparatively few goals I did get were away from home, and Anfield, once such a scoring paradise for me, seemed to have become my unlucky ground.

says
Roger Hunt
Liverpool

Sunday morning in the woods . . . a hard Saturday behind him. Hunt strolls with daughter Julie.

▲ Gift Book 1968–69

SO I POACHED OUR RECORD!

However, at long last I did manage to get the goal which broke that elusive record and believe me, I have never felt so relieved!

It came at Chelsea on January 18— a match we won 2–1—AND I AM NOT ASHAMED TO ADMIT THAT I POACHED IT.

It came like this: PETER THOMPSON made ground with the ball to the edge of the box and shot hard. Chelsea's reserve goalkeeper, TOMMY HUGHES, failed to hold the ball, let it slip loose, and I nipped in to prod it to one side of him and then clip it into the net.

Apart from my elation at having cracked that record I was almost as pleased because the goal put us ahead—and everyone gets special pleasure from getting a goal away from home.

For the record, that memorable game at Stamford Bridge was my 376th League appearance.

At that time, I had also netted 18 F.A. Cup goals, 16 more in European competitions, five in the Football League Cup, three for the Football League XI and 18 for England, making a grand total of 294 which would have set me in sight of the Jimmy Greaves feats—except that Jimmy chose last season—one of my poorest from a scoring viewpoint— to regain all his old goal flair.

I found it hard to score at home.

That is because teams playing away from home nowadays mark so much more tightly and frequently pull back eight men into defence, looking all the time for a draw.

Consequently, the penalty area becomes jam-packed and the openings fewer because there is hardly room to get sight of the goal, let alone spot a shooting gap.

In fact, we found it easier to score in our away games last season because with the home side exerting pressure on us we found we had more room to move in attack.

It seemed to me that it was the men coming from behind who were the most dangerous and a good case in point was West Bromwich Albion's TONY BROWN who is theoretically a wing-half and yet often comes in on the blind side in a " striker " position to get vital goals for the Midlanders.

Of course, the fact that Tony began as a winger has something to do with this for the ability to instantly assess a scoring situation must come naturally to him.

On the other hand, if we can get a goal up fairly quickly the situation changes again because our opponents then have to come out to try for an equaliser and again, we can find more space up front.

This is the way things are in this age of defensive football—it is not enough to keep pressing in the hope of " bulldozing " a goal in—you have to lure your opponents into traps and use one of your least marked players as a surprise striker.

It was this sort of situation which

happened at Chelsea in my record-breaking game—they had us packed back in defence and it was Peter Thompson who made the quick break, with me snatching the goal.

I have been asked many times my favourite method of scoring. Well, there is no definite " method " as such—you tend to take them as they come! I feel just as pleased with a " tap in " goal as I do with a spectacular run and shot. They all count the same.

I'm not a great player in the air as a rule and, looking back, I suppose that many of my goals have come off a ball flicked on to me by someone else's head or deflected to me from a colleague's foot—these are the chances I am always looking for—especially in the six-yard box when the ball can be in the net before a defence knows quite what's happened.

But I like to be in the game all the time, and feeling that I am contributing something towards it. At Liverpool, we have a very fluent attack with everyone capable of scoring.

Wingers IAN CALLAGHAN and Peter Thompson are always on the look out for goals, and so, too, is our " new boy " ALUN EVANS who last season slotted in some good goals for us.

IAN ST. JOHN, once such a prolific scorer for the Reds, doesn't manage so many now because very often he is playing a deep-lying role for us—and very effectively he does the job.

Going back to my own scoring feats, however, it was strange that up to the 1967–68 season I hadn't scored at all against Manchester United. It was just one of those things.

In 1967–68 I put the record right by getting two against them—one at home and one away. I also recall getting one of my best goals against Leicester City, another " bogy " side, in a F.A. Cup Sixth Round tie on our way to winning the trophy in season 1965.

Another goal which really delighted me was the fourth in Liverpool's magnificent 5–0 win over Arsenal in 1964 when we clinched the League championship before a full house at Anfield.

Two years later I got both goals in our 2–1 win over Chelsea—a game which ensured us the 1966 League title. Admittedly, I had a little luck with both goals for Chelsea's goalkeeper—in that match it was John Dunn, now with Aston Villa—got his hands to the ball on both occasions.

Curious that in two memorable games against Chelsea on neither occasion was Peter Bonetti in his usual spot between the posts.

In each of those League championship campaigns I scored over 30 goals and in our Second Division promotion season which preceded them I netted 41. That was in 1961–62.

I have had several hat-tricks in matches but my highest tally in one game was the four I slammed in against Stoke City on Boxing Day, 1963, when we won 6–1 and the Kop crowd had a real bean-feast. I scored all my goals in the second-half that afternoon—two with my head and two shots.

Sure, goals are my business but they seem to be getting harder and harder to get nowadays.

Perhaps if the trend swings back again to old fashioned attacking football I might be able to think in earnest about chasing that Jimmy Greaves tally and also (if I'm lucky) that wonderful aggregate League record of 434 set up by Arthur Rowley.

Hunt about to be swamped by team-mates after breaking Liverpool's club goal record.

January 1969 ▶ | April 1969 ▶ ▶

FOOTBALL MONTHLY

ROGER HUNT
Liverpool

BILL SHANKLY . . . the man
who leads the Anfield
bid.

LIVERPOOL CHASE A RECORD

Pace-setting Liverpool will
chalk up a Football League record
if they win the Championship
this season . . . it will be their
eighth title. Here (right) are the
men who hope to do it: (Back)
Graham, Clemence, Strong,
Lawrence, St. John. (Middle)
Wall, Smith, Byrne, Lawler, Evans,
Ross. (Front) Callaghan, Hunt,
Yeats, Thompson, Hughes.

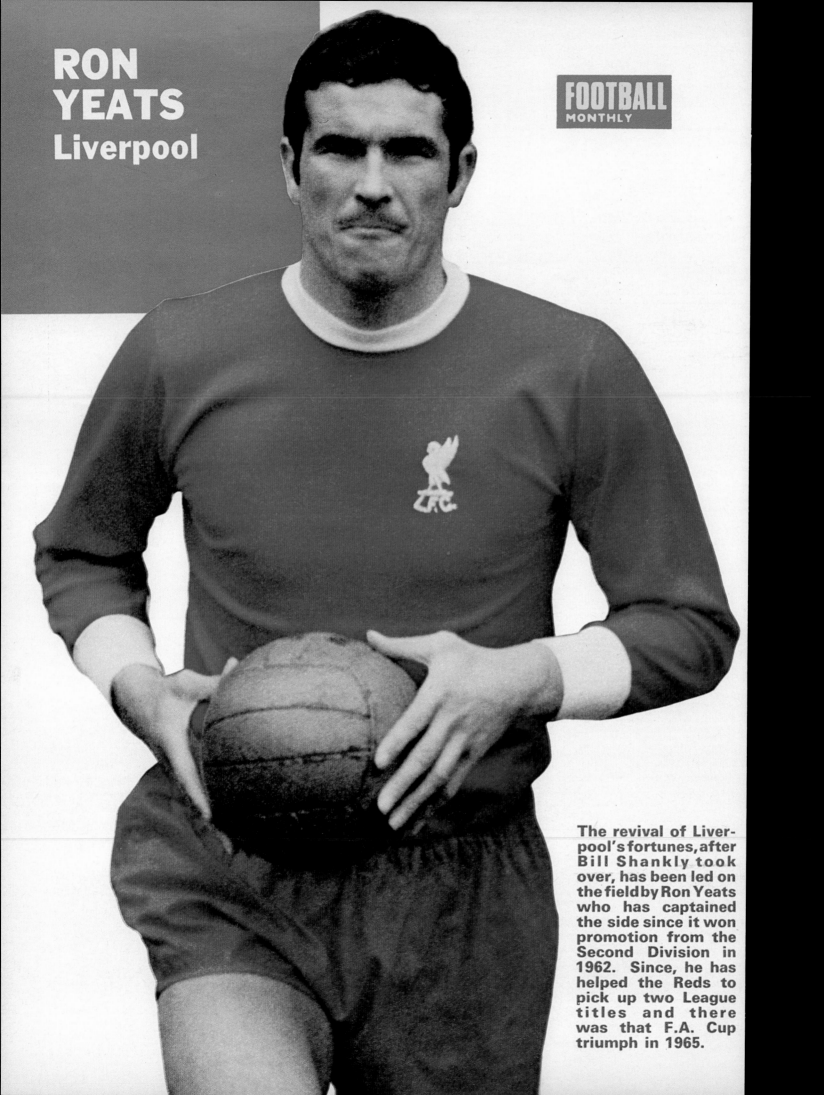

RON YEATS
Liverpool

FOOTBALL
MONTHLY

The revival of Liverpool's fortunes, after Bill Shankly took over, has been led on the field by Ron Yeats who has captained the side since it won promotion from the Second Division in 1962. Since, he has helped the Reds to pick up two League titles and there was that F.A. Cup triumph in 1965.

▲ November 1969

IN AND OUT BUT HAPPY

that's BOBBY GRAHAM, of Liverpool

by Peter Barnard

BOBBY GRAHAM makes more comebacks than you've had hot dinners—a slight exaggeration, perhaps, but that's how the man himself describes his in-and-out career with Liverpool. He isn't complaining, though, because being on the books at Anfield is a way of life and Bobby loves it.

This season he has been in the side since the first match. His performances have attracted much attention, with newspaper journalists descending on Anfield in the proverbial droves. The funny thing is that this so-called discovery is the most misunderstood player in the game.

Thousands of football fans are under the impression he is an 18-year-old whizz-kid who has suddenly emerged from the depths of Bill Shankly's stable to take the First Division by storm. Bob finds it pretty amusing.

The fact is he's 24, has been at Anfield for nine years and has played nearly 40 games in the first team. So he knows what it's all about and he knows that the rush of headlines mentioning his name is nothing worth getting excited about. *In other words, he's level headed.*

Most people in football have short memories, which is why most people have forgotten that Graham played for Liverpool in the first three games of last season and was equally impressive. Then an ankle injury put an end to his run.

"I was out for weeks," he says, "then I came back but the injury returned. So the boss bought Alun Evans from Wolves."

It's ironic, then, that when this season started, it was the £100,000 Evans who made way for Graham, who cost the club not a farthing.

He joined them as a 15-year-old (nine years ago, to save you working it out!) when farthings were still in being. It came about like this:

"I was playing for an amateur team in Motherwell—my home town—and I scored two goals in the Under-16 Scottish Cup Final. Two Liverpool scouts were watching. They asked me to come for trials and I signed for the club after those."

Graham had more than the obvious reason for joining Liverpool. When he used to stand on the terraces at Motherwell they had a player who became Bob's idol. A goal scorer he was—and in those days Motherwell scored an awful lot of goals.

Graham's connection with this player is now somewhat more direct, because they both play in the same team. And this other player, supposedly "over the hill", is scoring a lot of goals this season, like Graham.

Ian St. John is the name.

Said Graham: "I worshipped Ian at Motherwell and he is still something of a hero figure to me. I'll never forget my debut for Liverpool—it was against Aston Villa, and I scored a hat-trick. Ian was delighted, but what I remember most is that he kept urging me on to get a fourth. That's the kind of guy he is."

Graham went to Liverpool as a right-winger, but when he was in the reserves he started to play in midfield and then as a striker—his present role. He believes that playing in various positions, far from being unsettling, has helped him a

great deal. "But I like my present job best," he says, "because I suppose scoring is what it's all about. But I wouldn't mind being switched again—I don't really care where I play, just as long as I'm playing.

"The important thing is the team. Liverpool don't have individuals. Everybody works for the team. It doesn't matter who scores the goals, as long as they're scored."

This attitude answers the question: Why are Liverpool so successful? It's not that individual flair is submerged—far from it—just that individual flair must not be to the detriment of the team as a whole.

That also explains why Liverpool are not one of those clubs where transfer demands descend on the manager's office like toilet rolls on to many a pitch. "We're one big happy family," says Graham—and he really means it.

At some clubs, a player of his ability would have asked for a move long ago. He didn't, because . . . "I thought I could make the grade eventually. I loved being with the club and I married a Liverpool girl, so why should I move? It was better to fight for a place in the team."

Now the fight has been won—or so it seems—and Bobby can talk about his colleagues and his club as a senior player with considerable authority. A few examples:

ST. JOHN: "Everybody said the team were getting too old and, of course, Ian was the one mentioned most in that respect. We just laugh about it—you can't do anything else the way he's playing this season. We're always saying 'hey, Ian, here's your pension book'—that's how we look at it."

YEATS: "What a player Ron is! He's another one who was supposed to be cracking up, but he's as solid as ever in that defence."

SHANKLY: "What can you say about the boss? He's great—he makes everybody in the club feel like a million pounds, even when we've just lost. You couldn't find a better manager."

THE ATMOSPHERE: "As I said, it's tremendous. We're always laughing and joking. That doesn't mean we don't take the game seriously—of course we do. But

take training: it's enjoyable because it's varied and there's always a bit of light relief. We usually have a five-a-side game to round off a session."

It's funny, but to hear Bobby Graham talk you'd think he had been a First Division superstar earning vast sums of money all his life. It just goes to show that money and constant success is one thing, but happiness is something else again. HAPPINESS, IN FACT, IS BOBBY GRAHAM.

SPURS HELD BY THE LIVERPOOL RED GUARDS

"It's all yours," say Liverpool's Emlyn Hughes and
Geoff Strong as the ball goes through to 'keeper
Tommy Lawrence. And behind that last Liverpool
barrier fallen comrades can look back in the sure
knowledge that this Tottenham attack has come to
nothing.

THE 'BACK-ROOM' BOYS ARE

So far as Soccer-mad supporters are concerned, the "team" — those eleven highly-trained athletes chosen by the manager, who don the familiar jersey and take the field for each game — is all that matters.

How often, I wonder, do they stop to think of the other—smaller and much less publicised—"team" which operates not only on match days or during the season, but, led by the club secretary, is on-duty throughout the whole year?

My own "team" is a typical example, for as secretary of Liverpool F.C., I am responsible for the administration of a business with a turnover of something like half-a-million pounds each year!

While the manager and his team are constantly in the spotlight of Press, radio and TV coverage, little appears to be known of the pressures, stresses and strains that are imposed on those whose job it is to look after the business side.

And while I am not looking for kudos, or any of the glamour which one associates with this great national game, one thing is certain—that no club could ever hope to be successful without backroom organisation at least equal to that of the most successful commercial business in the land.

To leave the manager free to concentrate exclusively on team matters, the club secretary and his staff have to shoulder *all* the many duties and responsibilities that have to be dealt with if the club, as a business, is to run smoothly.

At Anfield on match days alone it is my job to ensure that apart from the permanent staff, 150 part-time workers are engaged and at their various positions—be they gatemen, programme sellers, stewards, or in the refreshment bars which, in our case, are controlled by a catering manager.

But this is only *one* of the six full days-per-week that the secretary and his staff put in at the ground.

With my assistant, Bill Barlow, who has been at Anfield for 12 years, and two girl clerks we are responsible for all the considerable office work—paying wages, ordering and distributing tickets and programmes, and looking after the shoals of correspondence.

We receive several hundreds of letters every week asking for information to settle bets, requesting club badges, players' autographs, back numbers of programmes, from visiting supporters asking for directions to Anfield, from home fans asking for directions to away grounds, plus the normal club business letters.

They all have to be answered in addition to arranging board meetings, committee meetings and travel for our *four* teams—including European

says PETER ROBINSON, secretary of Liverpool

travel, of course. It is also our job to establish and maintain a close liaison with local and national Press. Our attitude to Press publicity is very simple. We believe that the fans who pass through the turnstiles are our VIPs. They are the customers without whom there would be no Liverpool Soccer club.

They are entitled (within limits, of course) to know what is going on and we do our best to ensure that they receive all the information they require to satisfy their curiosity and to retain their interest in the club.

And in return we receive a loyalty that is second-to-none in the whole of the game.

To cope with all this behind-the-scenes activity, we are at our desks from 9 till 5, Monday to Saturday, with plenty of our spare time devoted to the cause.

We also have to arrange for the maintenance of the ground, apart from the pitch itself which comes under the jurisdiction of the manager and his groundsmen.

For this purpose we have a maintenance staff of three, plus six cleaners, who look after the day-to-day repairs. Major repairs, replacements, repainting and rebuilding go to outside contractors.

Accounts have to be kept, prepared monthly for the Board, and annually for the auditors.

Comes the end of the season, but not for us the two-or-three-month break that players (and spectators) enjoy. In fact, the close season is probably the busiest sustained period in any football club offices!

First of all, we have to send out renewal forms to each of our 14,500 season-ticket holders, advising them of any changes in prices of tickets. We allow them approximately one month to reply then we have to issue the new season's tickets which means dealing with something like £100,000 in cash. During that time

in sheer self-defence, we have to bring in four extra staff.

This takes six weeks of concentrated effort—after which we receive the following season's fixture lists for our four teams. Immediately, we have to get down to the task of making all the necessary travel and hotel arrangements for the whole of the programme.

By then the players are reporting back for early training, and any alterations or re-furbishing of dressing rooms, dining room, players' room, medical room, just have to be completed.

Home travel is, of course, a routine, pre-season job, but during the season if the club are involved in F.A. Cup or European games, the pressure on the administration department can become very intense.

An example was our away game in 1967 against Hungarian side Ferencvaros in the Inter-Cities Fairs

"Can I get my money back, if I'm not satisfied?"

Cup. We were notified of the draw in November—the game to be played before the end of December.

As most Eastern European grounds are snowbound in December it became essential to fix the date as soon as possible, and we agreed a date with the club that gave us just two weeks to make all the necessary travel arrangements.

Players' passports were checked, hotel rooms booked, air tickets organised, but in this case visas were necessary, and it normally takes a minimum of two weeks for these to be obtained.

We contacted the Hungarian Embassy, in London, who pulled-out all the stops, my assistant Bill Barlow travelled to London and literally sat on the steps of the Embassy until the visas were produced. This time we were lucky—we obtained them in just two days.

We also had to arrange to obtain presents for the opposing club—part of European Soccer. In this case we presented Ferencvaros with an inscribed silver salver, and the players, referee and linesmen with electric shavers. In return we received dolls dressed in national costumes and boxes containing six small bottles of local wines.

We also come under heavy pressure when F.A. Cup replays occur. We normally have a maximum of three days in which to allocate tickets to season-ticket holders, and if, as usually is the case, it is an all-ticket match, we have physically to hand over via the paybox, anything up to 54,500 valuable pieces of printed card. It sounds easy when one says it quickly, but believe me the organisation behind it, is tremendous.

Make no mistake, our backroom "team" is under just as much pressure as are those lads on the field, and—as in their case—success is a very satisfying experience.

DEDICATION

That's what is demanded at Anfield—and we've got it, says GEOFF STRONG of Liverpool

"Once a northerner—always a northerner" is a very true saying—and is one reason why, despite having spent six years in London with Arsenal, I am extremely happy at Liverpool, which is a bit nearer to my north-eastern birthplace.

My wife never settled in the "big smoke," which is why we were both very happy when the call came from Liverpool, and the transfer made.

But apart from preferring the north country, I find the Anfield set-up *so* professional. As in any sport or business it starts at the top and the ultra-professionalism of the boss, Mr. Bill Shankly, quickly rubs off on to players.

Before anyone can call himself a Liverpool player he first has to be completely dedicated to the team and to the club. Hence it follows that once accepted, you become one of a team of professionals in the strictest sense.

Which also—despite the seriousness of the game—makes it a happy club. There is a spirit of comradeship in the side which can come about only when a number of people are devoting all their energies to one common end, and placing the utmost reliance in each other. This is what makes—a team!

By all of which you will gather that I have been very much influenced in my career by Mr. Shankly, but long before I arrived in Liverpool, another gentleman had a profound effect on my future.

He was my headmaster at Newburn Hall School at Kirkheaton, near Newcastle, where I was born. His name was Mr. Bob McAndrews and he was—to put it mildly—a football fanatic.

He was the driving force behind the school team in which I played at wing-half—I also played twice for Northumberland County Boys at inside-forward.

When I left school at 15 I took up an apprenticeship

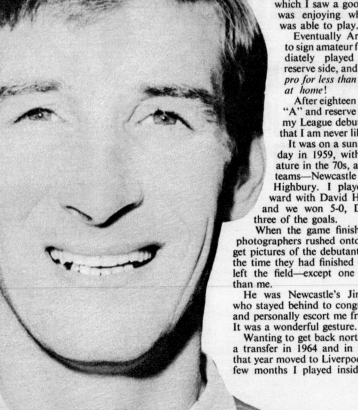

as a machine-tool fitter with a local firm and forgot about Soccer. I didn't even kick a ball for eighteen months, until I joined night classes and found that my instructor was—Mr. McAndrews!

He really gave me some stick when he discovered that I was not playing football and arranged for me to join Throckley Juniors where (playing wing-half) I soon found myself skipper.

At 18 I had passed the age limit for Throckley and joined Stanley United in the Northern League, playing against such famous amateur clubs as Bishop Auckland, Crook Town, etc., at centre-forward.

This League has always been a great recruiting ground for League clubs and scouts were regularly watching us play.

I had offers from Wolves and Middlesbrough, among others, and was invited to Molyneux for a week of trials, but returned home after one day.

I wasn't just playing hard to get—I was doing well at my job in which I saw a good future, and was enjoying what Soccer I was able to play.

Eventually Arsenal got me to sign amateur forms—immediately played me in the reserve side, and *at 19 I signed pro for less than I was earning at home!*

After eighteen months in the "A" and reserve teams I made my League debut in a manner that I am never likely to forget.

It was on a sunny September day in 1959, with the temperature in the 70s, against—of all teams—Newcastle United at Highbury. I played inside-forward with David Herd at No. 9 and we won 5-0, David getting three of the goals.

When the game finished the Press photographers rushed onto the pitch to get pictures of the debutant boy, and by the time they had finished everyone had left the field—except one player other than me.

He was Newcastle's Jimmy Scoular who stayed behind to congratulate me—and personally escort me from the pitch. It was a wonderful gesture.

Wanting to get back north, I asked for a transfer in 1964 and in November of that year moved to Liverpool where for a few months I played inside-forward, in

▲ March 1970

and out of the reserves and the League side.

The following May Liverpool were due to play Leeds United in the F.A. Cup Final at Wembley. Unlucky Gordon Milne went down with an injury, I got his place, we won 2-1, and I spent the following season battling with Gordon for his position.

And what a season (1965-66) it was for Liverpool! As Cup-holders, we reached the final of the European Cup-Winners' Cup (I scored the winning goal *v*. Celtic in the semi-final) and, of course, won the League title.

Unfortunately, I missed the final due to a cartilage operation—a game which

we lost 2-1 to Borussia Dortmund — but the Championship was fair consolation.

I played the full season in 1966-67, about half each at inside-forward and wing-half and when in October of the following season Gerry Byrne was injured I was asked to play left-back, more or less as a stop-gap.

I held the position right up to this season when iron man Tommy Smith was injured and I took over his duties as sweeper—which gave Peter Wall his chance on the flank.

As for the future. When I finish playing I don't think I shall stay in the game. I am already in partnership with a local

JIMMY SCOULAR (left) . . . stayed behind on the pitch to congratulate Strong (in action, above) after his debut against Newcastle in 1959. A wonderful gesture; says Strong.

professional man Kevin Dooley in a very good business.

Starting from scratch, we now have a thriving furniture and upholstery business after only two years of operation. We have contracts with big stores and breweries for seating, carpets, lino and curtains. This will obviously be my future, *but I hope, not for a long time yet.*

SAVED BY ROGER'S PENALTY

DID you know that Ian Ure, former Arsenal, now Manchester United "iron-man" centre-half, started his Soccer career as a goalkeeper? He did—in the same schoolboy side in which I played at inside-right!

It was when we were attending Dailly Junior School, at Dailly in Ayrshire, that Ian and I played together. I later moved to Russell Street School until, when I was 12, my family moved down to Culcheth near Warrington.

I continued to play at inside-right while at Culcheth Secondary Modern School, where one of my team-mates, incidentally, was Roger Hunt. We left school together at 15, and played for a local side, Croft F.C., I at outside-left, Roger at inside-right, and Johnny Green (ex-Blackpool, now with Port Vale) at centre-forward.

After the war, conscription continued, and when our goalkeeper Johnny Gordon was called-up for National Service, we had no one to take his place. So I was "conned" into filling the gap, and only four weeks later I was signed as an amateur for Liverpool, having been spotted by one of the Anfield scouts, Mr. Tom Bush.

I went through the usual learning process of games in the Anfield "C," "B" and "A" teams until after 18 months I reached the grand old age of 17, signed professional forms—and played two games with the Central League side. *This was living!*

In 1959 Mr. Bill Shankly took over as Liverpool manager and immediately put me into the reserve team as deputy to League team 'keeper Bert Slater. But I never got a first-team game and when in 1961 Jim Furnell was signed from Burnley it was back to the "A" team.

I thought "this is my lot" but in the 1961-62 season Bert Slater was transferred to Dundee, Jim Furnell was unlucky enough to break a finger, and in September, 1962, I made my League debut v. West Bromwich Albion at the Hawthorns where we were beaten 1-0.

But I must have done all right, for since my debut I have missed only FOUR League games and have played in ALL the club's many home and European Cup-ties—except for two Fairs Cup games against Dundalk when the club gave Ray Clemence a couple of games. It's a record of which I think I can be proud.

Another record—and I can't make up my mind whether to be proud of this or not—is that I am one of the few Soccer players for whom *seven* years have elapsed between international appearances. My first cap (for Scotland, of course) was v. Ireland in 1962.

My next excursion into the international scene didn't materialise until last year (1969) when I was chosen twice—against Germany and Wales.

Which was undoubtedly very satisfying after so long an absence—but even this cannot be classed as the highlight of my career to date. *Whatever happens to me in the future, I don't think that anything will ever match the feeling when I saved a penalty in a League game at Anfield.*

The game was important for it was the last game of the 1963-64 season. Arsenal were our opponents—and Liverpool just *had* to win the game to take the Championship.

There was no score when the Gunners were awarded the fateful penalty. Before the game Roger Hunt had tipped me off that if they were awarded a penalty George Eastham would probably take it, and he usually shot for the right-hand corner.

George did. I took Roger's advice, dived—and saved it. And, of course, it is now history that we went on to trounce the London side 5-0, and claim the League's top honour. But I often wonder what the result might have been had Arsenal made that early break-through.

Good old Roger! A typical bit of Liverpool team spirit! Which is what makes it such a great club.

On the other side of the picture; a moment which stands out in my memory as my worst was in the game v. Milan in Italy, in the semi-final of the European Cup the following season.

With a 3-1 victory under our belts from the first leg at Anfield, we felt confident of holding out in the away leg. But Inter-Milan really turned it on.

We were trailing 1-0 when I picked up a perfectly harmless ball. I was calmly bouncing it in the penalty area preparing to clear up-field when Peiro, their centre-forward, came from behind me, took the ball out of my hands with his left foot and cracked the ball into the net with his right.

I could have dug up the pitch with rage and frustration as this made the overall scores level. And what's more we went on to lose the tie on a 4-3 aggregate.

Thank goodness it was the final game of the season for Liverpool. At least I had the whole of the summer recess to get over my disappointment. But it certainly taught me a lesson—the hard way, too!

This is one Tottenham attack which will come to nothing. . . .

▲ April 1970

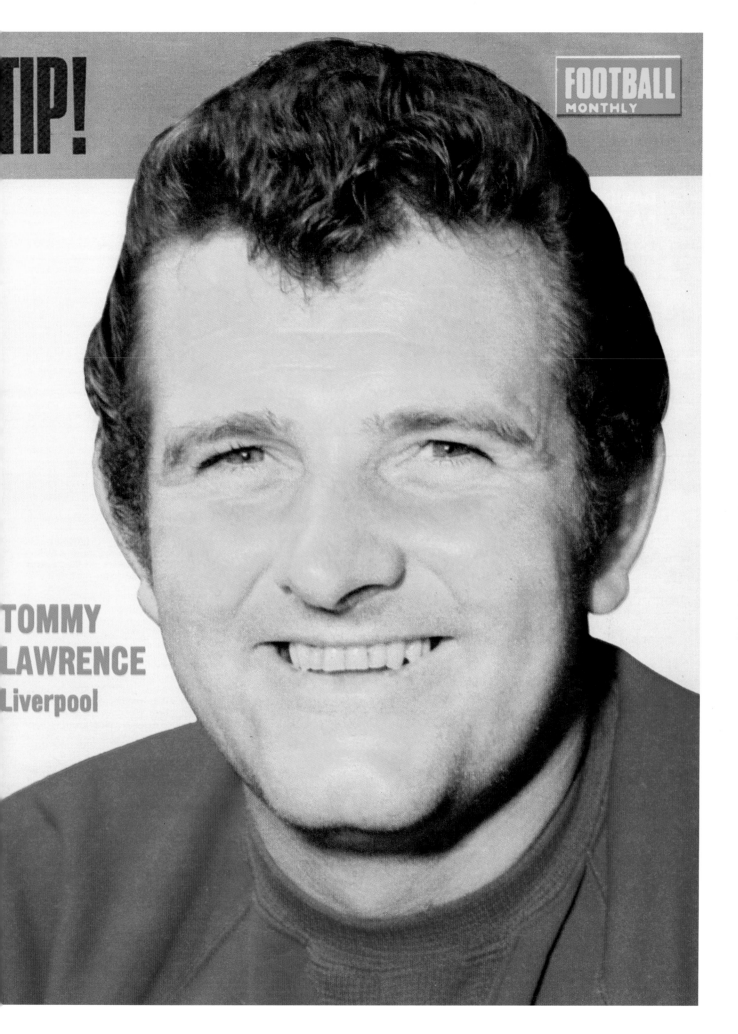

TIP!

FOOTBALL
MONTHLY

TOMMY
LAWRENCE
Liverpool

..a legend in his own lifetime...

LIVERPOOL were drawn at home to Fourth Division club Wrexham in the F.A. Cup last season. It seemed an unequal contest at first glance but football writers are forever searching for possible shock results at Cup-time . . . and several started to tip Wrexham as likely giantkillers.

On Merseyside in particular, and throughout the North in general, thousands of words were written in praise of Wrexham. So sweeping was the praise, so glowing the headlines, that the faint-hearted among Liverpool fans began to have doubts whether their favourites would survive.

Then, just 48 hours before the kick-off, one local reporter remembered to ask Liverpool manager Bill Shankly if he had anything to say about Wrexham.

" *Aye,*" said Shankly, " *I hope they turn up.*"

It was a characteristic come-back from a man who has become a Soccer legend in his own lifetime. Bill is acknowledged as one of the greatest personalities the game has known. Given the chance, most of us will tell our own special Shankly stories.

Many of them have, perhaps, been embellished with the passing of time . . . but all have the basis of truth. They are told, and re-told, with affection because anybody who can claim Shankly's friendship is proud of the fact.

Bill is aware of his own image. Sometimes, at an impromptu Press conference, he will make an outrageous comment because he knows it is expected of him. Yet with Bill staring them straight in the eye, few would dare to challenge his statement.

He has an intense passion for football and everything connected with it. His dedication to Liverpool is unswerving, but he was every bit as enthusiastic about Carlisle, Grimsby, Workington and Huddersfield when he managed those clubs.

Once, immediately after Liverpool had been defeated in a vital game, he was asked if he was disappointed.

Shankly, hardly able to believe his ears, regarded his questioner with scorn. " *Of course I am disappointed,*" he rasped, " *if you cut your finger, don't you bleed?*"

▲ Gift Book 1970–71

BILL SHANKLY

In Shankly's book it was as inevitable as that!

I could fill this article with Shankly stories. For instance . . . the suggestion that he stands by the Anfield entrance when a visiting team arrive and says in a stage whisper " *My, they are on the small side,*" or " *This lot look very young.*" Hardly the encouragement any players seek when about to face Liverpool and the Kop.

How, after one Liverpool victory which particularly gladdened his heart, Shankly was rumoured to have shaken the hand of each member of the opposing team as they dejectedly left their dressing room.

" *You played very well, but nobody could live with us when we are in that kind of form,*" Bill is alleged to have said.

But the folk-lore of Shankly never seems to give the full measure of credit to his ability as a manager. And Shankly is one of the greatest.

Liverpool are rightly acknowledged now as one of Britain's top clubs, and it is easily forgotten that they had spent five-and-half years in the Second Division when Shankly was appointed boss in December, 1959.

Few were the prophets at that time who imagined what a tremendous impact Bill would make at Anfield.

He had been an outstanding player in pre-war days, a wing-half with Preston North End and Scotland who lived only for the 90 minutes each Saturday. He didn't drink, didn't smoke, was early to bed and regarded defeat as a personal affront.

Shankly felt it an even greater indignity if he needed the attention of his trainer during a game. Yet, though seldom second best in a tackle, he took a full share of knocks.

A PROFILE
by
JOHN ANTHONY

Shankly and his players at a pre-season get together after Liverpool's F.A. Cup triumph in 1965.

Profile

BILL SHANKLY

Perhaps the supreme compliment to Shankly the wing-half comes from Peter Doherty, an inside-forward regarded as one of the finest of all time. " *I never met a player who relished the thought of opposing Bill,*" says Doherty.

The war took a chunk out of Shankly's career when he was at his peak, and he eventually put aside his boots at the age of 34 to go into management . . . then bitterly regretted his premature retirement from the field of battle.

" *I could have lasted several more seasons,*" he has insisted.

Then came the tough managerial " apprenticeship " of ten years before his Liverpool appointment. Bill had always felt he could achieve success with a big club and Anfield offered the perfect stage.

The potential was unlimited and the fans on the Kop were men after his own heart. They loved their football, and Shankly was determined to give them nothing but the best.

It was not something which could be done overnight. A season-and-half passed before Bill felt he had re-moulded the Liverpool team into a force capable of gaining promotion to the First Division.

When 1961-62 dawned Shankly had put his house in order. He had signed giant centre-half Ron Yeats to dominate his defence and take over as captain. He had the skilful Ian St. John up front to provide the missing link in attack.

These two Scots did everything Shankly asked of them—and Liverpool won the Second Division championship by eight points.

It was a perfect example of Shankly's shrewd judgment of players, and a year later he again demonstrated his ability to sign the right man at the right time by paying his old club, Preston, £40,000 for Peter Thompson.

Shankly had been on Thompson's trail for 18 months, and his knack in fitting together his team in jig-saw fashion was justified when Liverpool won the League title.

Thompson's skilful wing play on the left touchline contrasted perfectly with the hard running of Ian Callaghan on the right. And there was St. John to set up the chances . . . Roger Hunt to finish them off.

It was Liverpool's purple patch. The following season they gained their first-ever F.A. Cup triumph, and then won the championship again. They made their mark on the Continent by reaching the European Cup semi-finals and being unlucky extra-time losers in the Final of the Cup-winners tournament.

Liverpool's performances symbolised the self-belief of a Shankly team. Bill convinced himself that any player who wore a red shirt was the best in the world in that position . . . and, what's more, he had every player thinking the same way.

But there was more to Liverpool than confidence. Behind them was the great tactical know-how of Shankly who could combat the strengths of opponents and cash in on their weaknesses.

It is problematical whether Shankly will be able to re-create a Liverpool side in the Seventies to compare with the team who earned the constant Kop hymn of praise in the Sixties.

Yet he is a realist. While the old faithfuls of the first team were performing consistently week after week, Bill didn't neglect the grooming of their eventual successors.

When he felt the time had come for change, after an F.A. Cup defeat at Watford last February, Shankly started to inject the new blood. He has never been a man to live in the past and, at the age of 54, has proved the dynamo hasn't lost a single spark.

Now Shankly is singing the praises of his new-boys and planning fresh Cup and championship conquests. His belief that Liverpool will be tops again is as wholehearted as ever.

You couldn't tempt Bill from Anfield by offering him the job as manager of Portugal's Benfica or Spain's Real Madrid. He'll tell you " *I wouldn't go to either place . . . even for a holiday!*"

A Shankly-type grin as he walks off the Wembley pitch following the 1965 victory over Leeds. With him is Ron Yeats.

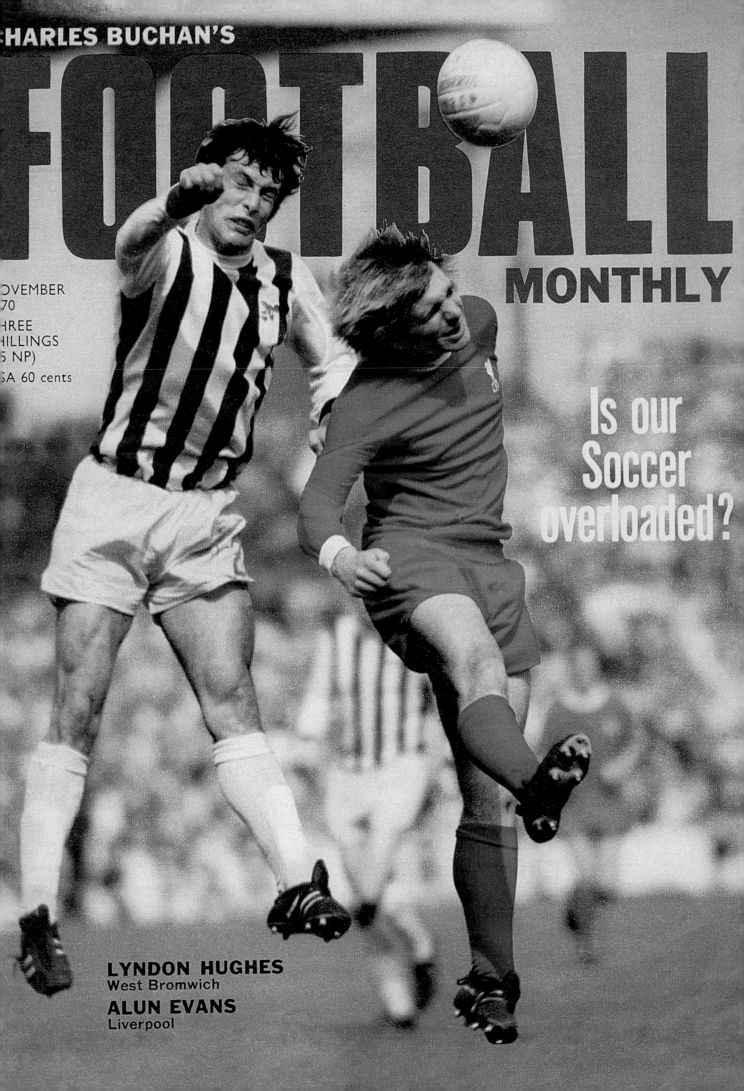

CHARLES BUCHAN'S

FOOTBALL
BALL
MONTHLY

NOVEMBER
70

THREE
SHILLINGS
(5 NP)
USA 60 cents

Is our
Soccer
overloaded?

LYNDON HUGHES
West Bromwich

ALUN EVANS
Liverpool

SIX MONTHS AND I WAS IN!

says STEVE HEIGHWAY, Liverpool

WHO wouldn't enjoy being paid for playing football? Yet for almost ten years I only regarded the sport as a hobby!

I joined Liverpool as an amateur in April 1970 and only signed professional forms in July after achieving my first "goal"—a university degree (B.A. in Economics and Politics).

But please don't think I take my football lightly. I am devoting all my time and energy to the game. At present it is my whole life.

My early and somewhat fairy-tale introduction to League Soccer happened because striker Bobby Graham unfortunately broke an ankle.

It is still my aim to lecture in Economics. In five or six years, I shall be an "old" man in the football world—yet I'll still have this teaching career to fall back on.

Meanwhile I am in a well-paid job, being kept at the peak of physical fitness and what's more —enjoying life! I look on it as a refreshing break after years of intense study which preceded my late entry into the game at 22.

Born in Dublin of English parents (hence my being awarded three International caps so far for the Republic!) I didn't play any football in Ireland as a boy. When I was ten, my family moved to England and at 12 I was playing rugby at Moseley Hall Grammar School at Cheadle, near Manchester.

I also played football for

STEVE HEIGHWAY . . . plans a teaching career when he quits the game

But they were—and particularly Tony Waiters, then a coach at Anfield, now back goalkeeping with Burnley. It was on Tony's recommendation that I eventually joined the list of famous names at Anfield. Then things really started to move!

After five games with the Central League side, I found myself in the party of 13 for the game against Burnley! Being 13th man must have been lucky for me!

For when Bobby Graham unfortunately dropped out, I was handed the No. 9 shirt for the League Cup game against Mansfield.

At the time of writing I've only scored one League goal against Burnley at Anfield. Although I should have notched two against Spurs at White Hart Lane.

It was a tremendous thrill to play on this fine ground and although Spurs beat us 1-0 we played extremely well and should have won. We would have done had I taken two chances that came my way. The first was when I lobbed the ball over the keeper's head—and inches over the bar and the second when I shot over again. This latter chance I should certainly have taken. Perhaps one can blame my lack of experience!

I learned a lot from the two games I played against Dinamo Bucharest in the Fairs Cup. Their keep-ball tactics were new to us and we had to do a lot of running to secure the ball once they were in possession.

Bramhall in the Lancashire and Cheshire League—usually on the right wing. During this period I played my first representative games for Cheshire Grammar Schools and for England Grammar Schools against Wales and Scotland.

At 17 I signed amateur forms for Manchester City, and spent three years at Maine Road on and off—because at 19 I left Moseley Hall to continue my studies at Warwick University.

At Warwick I played three times (still on the wing) for English Universities — and for British Universities on a tour of Belgium and Holland.

Because I wasn't always available for City owing to my

studies at Warwick, I played chiefly in the "A" team with occasional outings with the reserves.

The manager of the Universities Athletic Union (which ran the British Universities side) was Roy Rees—a lecturer in physical education at Liverpool University, and also manager of famous amateur club Skelmersdale United.

It was he who finally persuaded me to join "Skem" when I was 21, and it was here too that I first took on a striking role.

In view of past discoveries, the club has always attracted scouts, but I had no idea anyone was watching me.

Graham . . . his injury gave Heighway his big chance

Waiters . . . he recommended Heighway to Liverpool

EMLYN'S ENGLAND CALL GAVE ME BIG CHANCE

says Liverpool teenager
JOHN McLAUGHLIN

JUST a year ago I was a hopeful 17-year-old feeling quite chuffed that I was holding down a place in Liverpool's Central League side.

As the 1970-71 season moves into its second half, I find myself — amazingly — appearing regularly with the League side, playing with and against some of the top names in Soccer.

The big break came at the end of last season. Liverpool's concluding game was against Chelsea at Stamford Bridge and with Emlyn Hughes away on England duty I wondered if, being No. 6 in the reserves, I might have the chance to make my League debut.

Despite my secret hopes it was still a big thrill when I was told that I had been chosen. It was a very happy climax to two full seasons in the reserves.

It was in the opening game of the 1968-69 season, when I was only 16, that I was given my first game with the reserves. This too was at a famous ground —Villa Park.

My clearest memory of this game is the fact that it was a very hot August day, and I don't think I had a particularly good game. But I must have impressed someone for I retained my position,

Talking of position—I always played centre-half at school, at both St. Lawrence's Junior and at St. Kevin's Secondary Modern, in Kirkby.

My family moved to the new town from Liverpool, where I was born, when I was two. Needless to say I was always a keen supporter of the Reds!

In my last year at St. Kevin's I played five times for Lanca-shire Boys and on the recommendation of my games master I joined the Anfield staff immediately I left school at 15.

I never got the chance to play centre-half again. Right from the start I was given a midfield position which I still hold, wearing the No. 10 shirt.

I found League football altogether a different proposition after my experiences in the reserves. The game is much harder and there is far more pressure.

But, on the credit side, one is playing with better players— *the* best in fact—who can always be relied upon to help out when needed.

There is also the tremendous difference in atmosphere, the greater air of excitement and urgency, and European football is something different again.

Although I had already played for Liverpool against Ferencvaros in the Fairs Cup, the game at Anfield against Dinamo Bucharest in the next round was really special.

Although we won 3-0 (and eventually the tie 4-1 on aggregate) it was well into the second half before we scored the first of the goals we needed to take to Rumania for the second leg.

Talking of goals, I was fortunate enough, despite playing in midfield, to get a couple myself in my third appearance of this season.

This was at home against Huddersfield Town. Each came from a free-kick and each time I had taken up a position on the edge of our opponents' penalty box.

And although I am naturally right-footed I scored both goals with my left.

Above: John McLaughlin. Below: Emlyn Hughes

TOMMY SMITH– SHANKLY'S KEY TO THE NEW LIVERPOOL

ONE of the key men in Liverpool's apparently endless ability to march on from strength to strength this season has been Tommy Smith. And he has been one of the players most affected by the transition through which Liverpool have passed. For on his shoulders has fallen the responsibility of captaincy.

The transition began last season, and has been continued this season—and it has been effected successfully by manager Bill Shankly, despite the grievous injury blows which have struck down players such as Alec Lindsay, Ian Callaghan, Alun Evans and Peter Thompson.

New players have been drafted in; players largely untried in First Division football. And they have passed the test of fitness, stamina and ability. But Tommy Smith, perhaps, is the man who has passed the greatest test of all.

Through the 1960's the giant Ron Yeats was Liverpool's centre-half and captain. But when Shankly began to refashion his team Yeats, along with other stalwarts like Ian St. John and Tommy Lawrence, was a casualty. Smith was given the dual role of guiding the younger, less inexperienced players, and of raising his own game to inspire the men around him.

There was a new goalkeeper, Ray Clemence; a new centre-half, Larry Lloyd; a new left-back, Alec Lindsay. But Smith remained remarkably composed as the critics forecast gloom and despair for the new-look Liverpool. And it showed in his play.

So much so that those who had been predicting that it would take two years or more

Smith ... inspires the men around him

for Liverpool to become a First Division force again had to admit that here was a defensive unit which could be compared to the great defence of the 60's.

By the turn of the year Shankly was proclaiming: "We've got the best defence in Britain." And there were few who were disposed to argue with him.

Shankly points to Tommy Smith and says, emphatically: "If this lad goes out of the game without having won an England international cap it will be an injustice—a disgrace.

"Week after week this season he has played like a true captain —inspiring by example, defending tenaciously and yet with complete composure and skill. There is no one in the game better at doing the job he has been doing for Liverpool.

"Tommy Smith deserves international recognition, in the role he has been playing for us. It will be nothing but an injustice from the game itself if he has to hang up

Bill Shankly . . . "an injustice if Smith does not win cap"

▲ March 1971

SHANKLY'S KEY TO THE NEW LIVERPOOL

his boots without having won at least one international honour."

Smith, indeed, has been playing some magnificent football at the back. Whenever opposing forwards have threatened to break through, Smith has been around to do the sweeping-up.

And Shankly makes no bones about something else. "Larry Lloyd has proved himself to be a tremendous centre-half, worthy of the representative honours he has won in his first full season in the First Division. But Larry would be the first to admit that he has benefited enormously from having Tommy Smith by his side."

Smith has been a joy to watch; a skipper who has shed theatrical gestures and got on with the job in hand—playing football. He has produced polished displays, week by week; he has mopped up at the back, won the ball, and then set his own forwards in motion with judicious passes. And yet, through it all, he has lost none of the strength which always marked his play.

But the rough edges seem to have disappeared; there is the hallmark of class, where before, perhaps, physical endeavour was the most notable factor.

At the start of this season Smith had chalked up more than 220 League games for the Anfield club; almost 30 F.A. Cupties; and 33 appearances on the battlefields of Europe. Altogether he had scored 29 goals in 291 first-team games.

A hard man?—Yes. Last season, in a Fairs Cup-tie against Vitoria Setubal, of Portugal, he was Liverpool's star player . . . yet for all but 20 minutes of the game he played with part of a kneecap fractured. It meant that a player who had missed only eight of 204 previous matches was out of action for a month or so—a long time for Tommy Smith.

Earlier that month he had been a strong candidate for an England cap against Holland in Amsterdam when injury put him out of the running. Then the kneecap injury made him a non-starter for a place in England's line-up against Portugal at Wembley two weeks after that Fairs Cup-tie.

But this season "Iron Man" Smith has been back, driving Liverpool forward, week after week; setting an example by determined yet cultured play.

Bill Shankly never has been a man to sell his own players short. But his gravel-voiced praise of Tommy Smith is really a memo that England team manager Sir Alf Ramsey may well soon decide should not be ignored.

Stan Liversidge

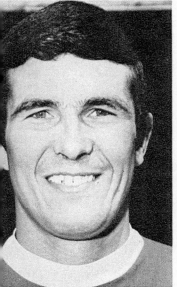

Ron Yeats (above) and Ian St. John (below) . . . "casualties" of the Shankly shuffle

Larry Lloyd (right) . . . owes much to Smith, says Shankly

The powerful, challenging stride of Emlyn Hughes, of Liverpool and England, is caught in this striking picture by staff photographer Ian McLennan

FOOTBALL MONTHLY

CHARLES BUCHAN'S

JUNE 1971   17½p   U.S.A. 70 cents

FOOTBALL
MONTHLY

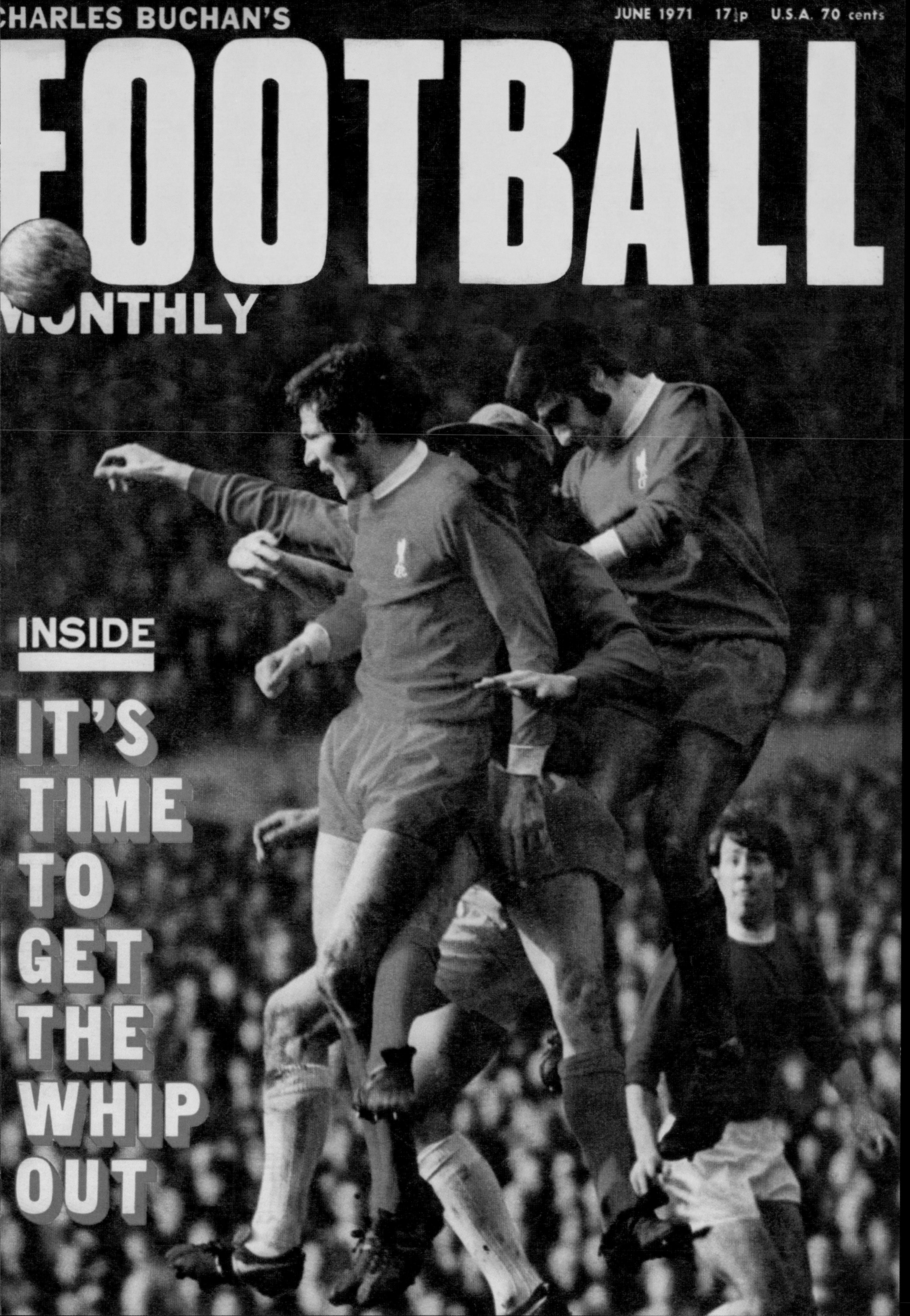

INSIDE

IT'S TIME TO GET THE WHIP OUT

HEIGHWAY

Heighway . . . explosive, courageous player with a flowing action

by BRIAN GLANVILLE

THE IMPORTANCE of being Heighway goes far beyond the fact that the young Liverpool striker was much one of the most exciting discoveries of 1970-71, an explosive, courageous player with a lovely, flowing action.

Still more germane is the fact that he, a university graduate, should instantly break through in First Division football after turning professional at the ripe old age of 22. Moreover, he did it with a club which prides itself on the intensity of its training.

It's especially pleasing, and ironic, to remember a chat with Bill Shankly, Liverpool's implacable manager, after one of Heighway's earliest matches, as a substitute, at West Bromwich.

I asked Shankly when he would be using Jack Whitham, for whom he'd paid Sheffield Wednesday £65,000 in the close season. "When he's fit enough for Liverpool!" Shankly retorted.

Yet Heighway, an amateur with Skelmersdale the season before, was fit enough for Liverpool within a matter of weeks!

His own explanation of this is intriguing and instructive. "I simply," he says, "went through the same thing as anybody else. Training is not a thing that lasts you for ten years; it lasts you for a season. When I started at the beginning of this season I was no fitter or less fit than anybody else."

He does, though, admit that the games were very hard at first: "I couldn't last the games at first, at all. Even if you train to a peak there's a question of knowing how to use it in a match."

The point is that if Heighway can do it, then so can others of his age and educational background. To put it another way, if Heighway can come through at 22, a ton of high explosive is detonated beneath the old, fond fallacy that boys must turn to a professional career at 15, or they will never make it.

I find it especially paradoxical that, during the very season that Heighway emerged so brilliantly, Alf Sherwood, the old Cardiff City and Wales full-back, should announce in an interview that Liverpool had told him to look for Welsh youngsters of nine years old—and under.

As competition grows ever sharper, as clubs fight more and more desperately for success, and for survival, it is perhaps inevitable that they should try to outflank one another by grabbing

▲ June 1971

HAS EXPLODED A MYTH

their players younger and younger. But from the point of view of the boy footballer, it is appalling; a disgrace and a blemish on our supposedly affluent society.

Boys of good intelligence, who in our post-war educational system might go through, like Heighway and Brian Hall of Liverpool, like Suddaby of Blackpool, to a university education, are side-tracked into what might easily prove a blind alley.

How many players, joining a professional club at 15, and giving up their formal education, find themselves out of the game at the age of 20? Or, at best, out of the League? And even if they remain in League football it may be only at a relatively ill-paid, Third or Fourth Division, level.

Moreover, the finest footballer must face the moment when he can no longer play, when he must turn to something else. The Heighways and Halls, with their degrees, will be immeasurably better placed than most.

Heighway is less pessimistic than I· "I think it important to look at the end product," he says. "There are very few down-and-out footballers at 30. They make so many contacts, they grow up so quickly. They've got the wherewithal to make a good living. There are plenty of avenues open to them, possibly more avenues than there would be for a B.A."

I remain a little sceptical, and even if Heighway were right, it still would not solve the problem of the "drop-outs" who have fallen between two stools.

Johnny Giles, Leeds United's Irish international, an intelligent young man who is clearly one of those who might have gone on to higher education, sees the problem as purely economic; clubs, he believes, just couldn't afford to wait so long for the late developer.

"If a player's not doing it by the time he's 18 or 19, there are other players on the staff who are 15. What kind of a staff would you have if you waited till every player was 22." As to Heighway: "His game is based on his physical powers; if he was a yard slower he wouldn't be a player at all."

Which is as much as to say that if Puskas hadn't got a left foot he wouldn't have been a player either.

But, even if one takes Giles' point, surely it makes it all the more significant that Heighway

came through at 22, *because of,* rather than despite, his physical attributes? Behind the myth that boys must take to the game at 15 lies a belief that if they don't they will never adapt to its demands of pace and stamina.

Arthur Rowe, that splendid former Spurs player and manager, now in charge of the Football Hall of Fame, told me: "I don't think it was ever true. I didn't go pro until I was about 20. If you've got enough ability it doesn't make any difference if you go at 15, 17. I think the ones that come through later have either got to have a tremendous amount of ability, or else they're late developers for some reason or another."

Tommy Cavanagh, the Nottingham Forest coach, on the other hand, points the moral of a tale of two young Scots professionals, one of whom went home for a year to complete his education, and has since lost ground, while the other has played in the Forest first team. You pay your money and you take your choice.

Mine is already taken. I believe that a lot of almost fetishistic rubbish is talked about when and how a professional footballer must commit himself to the game (and its long hours of idleness), about the alleged super-fitness of the modern player, and I believe that Heighway has gloriously exposed it.

Alf Sherwood (top) . . . asked by Liverpool to look for players of nine years old and under. Brian Hall (left), university-educated like Heighway, in action against Dave Wagstaffe of Wolves

Brian Hall bursts between Arsenal's John Radford and George Armstrong in the F.A. Cup Final at Wembley

NO ARGUMENT! WEMBLEY IS A KILLER

by BRIAN HALL Liverpool

MUCH is written about the electric atmosphere, tension and notorious muscle-racking turf of Wembley, but we at Liverpool get our fair share of atmosphere in every home game at Anfield. No body of people could be more enthusiastic, more encouraging, more vocal than the famous Kop.

So although I was thrilled when last May we faced the prospect of playing Arsenal in the F.A. Cup Final I was in no way overawed, despite my youth and comparative lack of experience in the top class.

As we marched out into the blazing cauldron I told myself that this was merely an extension of Anfield—bigger, with much more at stake than in a usual Saturday game.

My ideas changed when we began to play! I can now assure you that everything you have heard about the Wembley turf is 100 per cent true. Never has a game of Soccer been such hard work.

After almost a full season as a member of a top-class League side, in first-rate physical condition and trained for 90-minute games under almost any conditions, I was confident of my staying power. But how *that* turf tugged at my feet.

During the course of a game one normally moves into position always with something in reserve. But at Wembley the effort of getting into the required position was almost too much, with little energy then left to execute a move.

But I wouldn't have missed the experience for the world—despite the disappointment of losing. Now all I ask is to get back once again—this time to win.

Apart from this defeat at Wembley, last season was a great one for me. I had previously played only for 40 minutes, against Stoke City as substitute for Roger Hunt when he suffered an injury, when I was chosen for the Football League Cup game against Mansfield Town. Shortly afterwards I made my League debut against Southampton at The Dell.

Although I didn't know it then I was destined to hold my position for the rest of the season.

Perhaps I was lucky—for I had previously played many Central League games with Ray Clemence, Larry Lloyd, John McLaughlin and Alec Lindsay, who were already in the side. Their presence undoubtedly gave me confidence, and helped me a lot.

The Cup Final apart, the most memorable game of the season was the semi-final against our traditional foes—Everton. It marked a triple personal achievement.

The incident occurred when Alun Evans picked up the ball on the left and flipped it into the goalmouth. Goalkeeper Andy Rankin went up for it—so did our John Toshack—and the ball landed at my feet, ten yards out.

I hit it hard, Howard Kendall ran across goal in an effort to intercept but missed it, and into the net it went—marking my first goal for the senior side, a goal against Everton—and a goal against Everton *in an F.A. Cup semi-final*. What a great moment!

If ever one particular moment justified my decision to take up Soccer as a career this was it. And it is a decision I have never had cause to regret, although there was one occasion when I wondered just what I was letting myself in for.

I signed as an amateur for Liverpool while a student at Liverpool University. Once I had gained my B.Sc., I was offered and accepted professional terms, and in almost my first game after taking the plunge I was taught a lesson that I will never forget.

I was playing in a reserve game and an opposing full-back kicked me right up in the air very early in the game. I can assure you that I have never jumped so high in my life. He quickly realised that he had upset me, this put him right on top, and made the game a miserable one for me.

It worried me over the week-end, too, but I suddenly realised that this is what the professional game is all about. It taught me that though I am not a giant I would just have to stand up and defend myself. That full-back does not know it, but he helped make me a better player.

Now I don't worry how big or strong they are.

My energies are now all concentrated on holding my place in this fine Liverpool side, and my future ambitions are to get hold of that Cup-winners' medal, and to reach international status. *But for which country?*

I was born in Glasgow but my father is English and we moved to Preston when I was three months old and I was educated at Preston Grammar School and Liverpool University, so I am completely English.

▲ October 1971

Steve Heighway plays it clean.

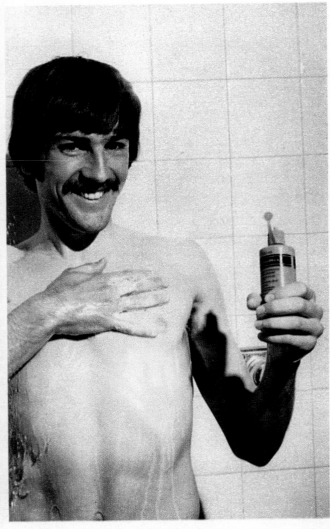

Steve Heighway, Liverpool and Republic of Ireland, B.Sc (Econ.) is a superstar at 22. He plays it clean — on and off the field. Steve knows the value of keeping in good physical shape. He relies on training, a balanced diet and pHisoHex.

pHisoHex is an antibacterial skin cleanser that surgeons all over the world rely on for germ-free hands both before and after

operations. And doctors prescribe it for spots and acne.

He knows that regular washing with pHisoHex together with thorough rinsing, will clean out the dirt, grease and germs that encourage spots.

Play it clean on and off the field with pHisoHex.

Like Steve Heighway.

pHisoHex at your chemist's.
For skin as clean as a surgeon's hands.
pHisoHex is a registered trade mark.

For a free copy of the Teenage Acne Booklet please write to: Mrs G. Usher, Winthrop Laboratories. Dept. FM1, Winthrop House, Surbiton-upon-Thames, Surrey.

▲ October 1971

NOW ANFIELD APPLAUDS A NEW MID-FIELD GENERAL...

LIVERPOOL have added a new dimension to the strength, power and will to win for which they have always justly been famed—and, in the process, have given a new lease of life to Peter Thompson who began his career as a left winger, played with equal success as a centre-forward, and this season has donned a No. 8 jersey to win new admirers.

Liverpool last season conceded only 24 League goals, to equal their previous best-ever defensive record. Today, manager Bill Shankly rates that tally as one which might stand as an all-time record. For the Reds of Anfield have revised their tactics. They switch with equal facility from 4-3-3 to 4-2-4, and back again . . . and Peter Thompson became a key man in this new flexible formation which brought goals flowing from the kick-off.

Thompson says: "When I wore the No. 11 jersey and played at outside-left, I was a 100-per-cent raider. I didn't HAVE to get back, to help out— my real function was to raid. This season, with a No. 8 on my back, I've been playing in the half-back line—and although I've been playing almost at right-half, I've still been able to go forward and attack, when the chance has been there.

"I've been the player who has turned a 4-3-3 formation into 4-2-4, dependent upon how the game has been going. I've been the man to break from midfield and give us four attackers; and I've been the front man whose job it is to go back and turn it into 4-3-3 again.

"I've found myself enjoying this role, too. It's hard work, of course . . . but no more tiring than when I was playing as a direct wing raider. In some respects it's easier. It's my fault if I don't get into the game, in this midfield role, for everything *happens* in midfield.

"*When you're out on the wing, you can fade out of the game for long periods. You can run and chase, go looking for the ball— and come off at the end having had very few kicks at it. But you still feel absolutely shattered! On the wing, you rely on so many people to get you into the game . . . and you can come off exhausted, yet still dissatisfied because you felt you never really got into the thick of things.*"

Thompson believes he has learned a great deal, too, from the role he has played. "The Boss says that great players know when to hold the ball and when to let it go. In the past I held the ball when I got it—and sometimes I found myself trying to beat a player I'd already beaten which made it doubly hard work.

"In midfield, I've got to use the ball a lot more—I've got to be prepared to release it. And as well as learning this, I've learned a great deal about positional sense. I'm conscious of the role I'm playing, conscious of where I am, where I should be, the need to release the ball for a telling pass."

The numbers game means nothing in football today, of course. Thompson No. 8, Steve Heighway No. 9, Ian Callaghan No. 11, Kevin Keegan No. 7 . . . yet Heighway often plays as a marauding winger, Callaghan has a midfield role, Keegan is a front man who's also able to drop back, if required.

Liverpool's new approach is based on their confidence in a fluidity of play which enables them to shrug off a goal scored against them—because they feel they can wipe out the deficit.

And they are not the only team to have introduced new facets into their play, this season. Thompson reminds you that Manchester United—who, like Liverpool, had scored a dozen goals after five matches—had men like Charlton, Gowling and Morgan creating, as well as going up.

Thompson has found that the ball players have been given greater freedom since referees stamped on the tackle from behind. "When I played on the wing, and was upfield with my back to goal, I used to have a defender right behind me. My legs were often black and blue at the back from defenders who were determined to let me know they were there.

"But recently, it's been the defenders who have been doing the moaning and the forwards who've been happy in the knowledge that they can take a pass and use the ball a bit without having to lay it off swiftly because they knew they were going to get a knee in the back. For my money, the defenders had it cushy for too long. It became increasingly easy for them, massing at the back.

"I must admit I feel the ball-playing forwards are being allowed to come into their own more, and I hope it's a ball-playing team which wins the title. And there ARE some around . . . Liverpool, Manchester United, Manchester City, Sheffield United. These are team who— given the chance—can play football and entertain. Since the clamp-down by referees, I reckon forwards have been able to take a pass with more confidence.

"Yes, I believe the ball-players are coming into their own, again —although whether, over a season, this is the type of Soccer which wins titles remains to be seen.

"*I'll admit I was surprised at the number of goals Liverpool had scored, after half-a-dozen matches. Last season, we*

Stan Liversedge analyses Liverpool's inter-changeable 4-3-3/4-2-4 tactics

▲ November 1971

PETER THOMPSON

❝On the wing you sometimes get hardly a kick❞

Kevin Keegan

dominated a lot of teams and gave away very few goals ourselves—but we didn't score many either. This season, we kicked off by dominating once more—and scoring goals, in the process."

Thompson is all in favour of footballers being allowed to play football—but he emphasises that forwards shouldn't be allowed so much protection that they can become casual and take it easy. "Soccer is still a man's game," he declares. "But it's certainly been a good thing to cut out this kicking at the back of the legs.

"Believe me, I've worked even harder than I did in the past . . . but, somehow, I haven't felt any more tired. I've been doing more running, but less on the ball. When you're winning, or when you're playing well, you feel you could carry on for ever. It's when you've taken a hammering from a defender, and you've not been able to enjoy the game—that's when you walk off weary."

CHRIS LAWLER: QUIET IDOL OF THE KOP

THE FAMOUS KOP fans call him "Mr. Consistency". Legendary Liverpool boss Bill Shankly proudly describes him as "the perfect professional", and managers up and down the country point to him as Soccer's first gentleman.

The man they are all united in praising is modest England full-back star Chris Lawler.

In an era that elevates youngsters to stardom almost overnight, it seems a little ironical that only recently the many talents and qualities of Lawler have become fully recognised.

Perhaps his qualities and special skills tended to be devalued because he has managed to maintain such a high level of consistency throughout his career.

Any Anfield fanatic would have to stretch his memory and scratch his head to remember the last Liverpool line-up that did not include Chris Lawler in the No. 2 shirt—apart from that game last season before the Cup Final when Liverpool put out a team of reserves against Manchester City.

In fact the last time cool Chris missed a first-team match was back in October 1965, when injury kept him out of a Cup Winners' Cup tie with Juventus in Turin.

Since then Lawler has been an automatic choice in well over 400 first-team games . . . and has chalked up nearly 350 League appearances in that famous red shirt.

Rain or snow, home or away, in good times and bad, Lawler

▲ January 1972

by RAY BRADLEY

has held on to his No. 2 shirt to provide a nostalgic link between the great Liverpool side of the Sixties and the present Anfield line-up. A remarkable tribute to both his consistency and his determination.

Lawler himself is pushed to remember the last time he missed a match through injury, although he confesses there were quite a few times when he was doubtful because of knocks.

"I've had my fair share of knocks but I've always managed to get rid of them by the following Saturday," he claims almost casually.

"Most injuries are really in the mind. There's nothing like a good 90 minutes to dispel nagging worries about a sore calf muscle or a dodgy ligament. When the whistle starts you forget all about them and just get on with the game. But you do need a bit of luck to steer clear of serious injury. So I suppose I have been pretty lucky so far."

But it takes more than a down-to-earth attitude to set up such a phenomenal record in the hard world of the First Division, where the pace is hot, the stakes high and the pressures to maintain a high level of consistency almost intolerable.

When Liverpool were ravaged by injuries last season only sheer determination enabled Lawler to remain a solid back-four fixture in the best defence in the Football League.

Bob Paisley, cuts-and-bruises man at Anfield, pin-pointed that determination when recalling the last time Lawler was doubtful through injury last season.

Says Bob: "Chris came in every

Lawler uses his ability in the air against Norman Hunter (above) and below, second left, prepares for the Cup Final against Arsenal

...QUIET IDOL OF THE KOP

day for treatment—including sessions on Sunday—although he was hardly able to do any training for a month.

"But every Saturday he was out there on the field giving 100 percent and no one ever knew what a battle it had been to get him fit between games. The lad doesn't know the meaning of the word 'quit'."

Although the fitness and stamina of Lawler have cemented him as a pillar in the Liverpool defence, it is his skill and stealth more than his strength which elevated him to full England recognition last season.

A tall, graceful player who excels at the quick interception, he is a master at outwitting a forward rather than overpowering him.

Lawler has few peers at the art of turning defence into attack at the earliest opportunity. A skilled interception, a quick one-two with Tommy Smith, and Lawler is off on the overlap as soon as he spots an open space. Frequently his speed off the mark and ability to capitalise on a forward error has enabled him to suddenly appear in an unguarded spot to support his attack. And his renowned ability to sneak in on the blind side of an opposing defence and finish off a move with a surprise shot or a well-timed header has perplexed many a goalkeeper.

Nearly 50 goals in a full-back career spanning eight years are telling testimony to the lethal Lawler's ability as a goal-scoring full-back.

The attack-conscious Lawler possesses a powerful shot, brilliant heading ability, coolness and neat control on such occasions—all superb assets even for a recognised top striker. And Liverpool have made full use of such assets by encouraging his attacking flair.

Although modesty forbids Lawler to say so, it has now become an accepted practice for the tall defender to become an auxiliary forward in a team that have tremendous strength in depth but frequently disappoint because of their lack of goal-scoring power.

All those splendid Lawler goals are but an added bonus for a team that have become accustomed to relying on his skilled expertise in all aspects of defensive play.

In a side brimming with powerhouse defenders the delicate skills of Lawler provide a polished shield for his teammates and added argument for those who claim defenders do not have to have four rows of teeth to be effective.

Lawler's ability to keep his cool under pressure is one of the reasons he has now established himself as England's right-back—and not before time, some shrewd judges claim.

Such recognition was long overdue, claims his club skipper

Tommy Smith, and fulfilled a long-cherished ambition after the winning of England honours at schoolboy, youth and Under-23 level.

"It had always been my ambition to play for England at full international level," says Chris,

Lawler ... "few peers at turning defence into attack"

"but I honestly thought I had missed my chance last season.

"Then, out of the blue, I was called up for the squad against Malta at Wembley. I felt a bit nervous at first but luckily I settled in quickly and now have four full England caps."

England recognition may have come a little late for the 27-year-old Anfield defender, but, as usual, he has made the most of it to prove yet again his undoubted class. Yet Liverpool remains his first love.

Of the present side Chris claims: "We certainly have some wonderful young players . . . people like Steve Heighway, Ray Clemence and Larry Lloyd. And, of course, we've still got Tommy Smith, a player I have been associated with ever since schoolboy days.

"But even allowing for improvement as the side matures together we will have to go some to equal that great side of the '60s. But who knows with a man like Bill Shankly as manager. He has rebuilt Liverpool twice. Who's to say he won't make them great twice?"

Meanwhile Chris Lawler will just keep turning it on for the team he has idolised ever since he was a schoolboy. And if a few more England caps and a few more goals are added along the way it's just another bonus from the man every Liverpool fan has learned to call "Mr. Consistency".

The Kop has had many kings, but few, if any, have given more stalwart service.

Lawler at an England training session with clubmate Tommy Smith and Gordon Banks

May 1972 ▶

Alan Oakes (left) and goalkeeper Joe Corrigan
crowd out Liverpool ace Kevin Keegan this time, to the relief
of Tommy Booth, but Shankly's boys were on song
with a 3—0 drubbing of Manchester City

LARRY LLOYD

TOMMY SMITH

STAN LIVERSEDGE poses the question...

LIVERPOOL dominated the domestic Soccer scene in the mid-1960s as—in successive years—they scooped the First Division championship, the F.A. Cup, and the championship again. The years of 1964, 1965 and 1966 were golden, indeed, for Bill Shankly's men. But, inevitably, the team which did the damage to all the others was broken up—Stevenson, Milne, Byrne, Hunt, St. John, Yeats, Lawrence, Strong . . . these players went their ways.

As the stalwarts departed, there were reshuffles in the pack at Anfield. There were times, too,

when Liverpool did not seem to be the force they were. And yet —as Leeds manager Don Revie has so often said—you can never write off Liverpool. They carry on fighting when other, lesser mortals would have given up the struggle.

Two seasons ago, Liverpool were in more than just a transitional period; they had to cope with a list of injuries—and serious ones—as long as your arm. Experienced players, too, were put out of action for months at a time. And unknowns were thrust into the fray—men like Steve Heighway and Brian Hall. Heighway acknowledges: "In that season, it was a case of everyone giving all-out effort.

There wasn't really time to work out a style, a pattern."

But, despite their problems, Liverpool marched to Wembley, although they lost 2-1 against Arsenal in the F.A. Cup Final. Their skipper, Tommy Smith, was candid enough to admit: "Frankly, I didn't feel, at the start of the season, that we would do as well as we did."

Last season the Anfield faithful waited with eager anticipation for the signs of greatness— another run to Wembley, maybe, a successful tilt at the European windmill, or even the championship of the First Division.

Liverpool were up among the leaders, they were in Europe, they had the F.A. Cup in their

LIVERPOOL

▲ June 1972

EVE HEIGHWAY   EMLYN HUGHES   ALEC LINDSAY

sights. But, gradually, they began to stutter, and their horizons were narrowed considerably, as they went out of Europe, out of the F.A. Cup and—seemingly—out of the championship reckoning.

Three games around the turn of the year really hit them. They lost by the only goal at Leicester and West Brom, and they lost at home in the League to Leeds. The goals began to dry up. And then, without warning, Liverpool began to steam ahead once more . . . until, with but a handful of games to go, they had emerged as very real rivals to Leeds, Derby County and Manchester City for the title.

Steve Heighway summed it up

when he said: "We've been working to achieve understanding as a team, to know our roles and create a real blend. And, finally, it paid off." Now, during this close season, Soccer slumbers . . . but Bill Shankly won't have lost his interest in Soccer. Does he ever?

And, as the summer weeks go by, is he even now plotting for another takeover at the top? Not for a single success, but for a whole series of triumphs?

In short, are Liverpool destined to become the team of the 1970s, with their sights on League and F.A. Cup, and a plundering of the European honours?

In Ray Clemence, Liverpool

have a goalkeeper who falls little short of the immaculate Gordon Banks—and HE is tagged the world's No. 1. Liverpool have a shrewd skipper in Tommy Smith —"this fellow isn't just a hard player, he's got very real talent," proclaimed Shankly after Liverpool had beaten Everton for the right to meet Arsenal at Wembley.

Liverpool have Chris Lawler, cool and cultured as a full-back, menacing as an extra attacker, as his half-century of goals for his club amply demonstrates. They have Emlyn Hughes, another England man, and a powerhouse of a player who also can hammer the ball past a 'keeper.

They have worked on new-

comers Heighway and Brian Hall, and these two have shown that their first season wasn't simply a flash in the pan. They have in John Toshack a tall striker who can use his head—literally—when it comes to the art of unsettling defences and nodding home goals. And they have produced a player of immense potential in young Kevin Keegan.

For a time last season Steve Heighway found himself floundering as he sought to recapture form. Some may feel that next time out, Keegan will suffer, because opponents now know his style, and respect the menace he represents.

Manchester United goalkeeper

team of the 70s?

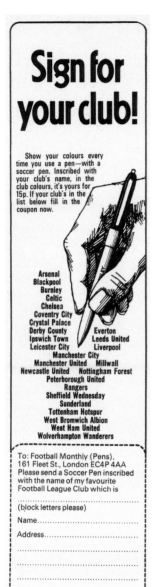

Back in the picture—Bill Shankly with Brian Hall and Alun Evans, whose semi-final goals took Liverpool to Wembley last year.

Alex Stepney has seen Keegan at close quarters. Stepney admits: "It's possible Keegan will find it more difficult. But good players show that they can still play, despite the pressure and the opposition—and this fellow has real flair.

"He's terrific in the air, possesses real speed—he must have been the bargain buy of last season at £35,000. On today's values you've got to assess him at between £100,000 and £120,000."

Scotland's supremo, Tommy Docherty, termed Keegan "the most exciting young player I've seen in English Soccer this season." Docherty paid this tribute but a few months ago. Another former Preston star, Tom Finney, could not speak too highly of Keegan, either. And Peter Doherty, Alan Ball's right-hand man at Preston, backs up the rating of Docherty and Finney.

Indeed, Peter Doherty feels a sense of grief, because Preston went in for Keegan when he was at Scunthorpe, but their price wasn't enough to tempt Scunthorpe—and Preston couldn't go any higher at the time. So Liverpool succeeded where Preston had failed . . . and Peter Doherty still muses: "Aye . . . the lad should have come to us." Although Doherty doesn't begrudge Liverpool their capture, and he does admit that if Keegan is to blossom still further there couldn't be any better academy of learning for him than Bill Shankly's Anfield.

A couple of seasons ago Bill

Shankly told me: "When I've got a team together which I think will take the title, then I'll say so." Bill hasn't said it yet—but he must be musing on the prospects for the next few seasons with a quiet sense of satisfaction.

Look at Liverpool all round, and what do you see?—Never less than a team of fighters, on any occasion. But there's more: Power, skill, heart, willingness to work for each other, youth and experience blending together. Plus flair.

Straight down the middle—and there's a backbone of strength, with Clemence and centre-half Larry Lloyd, backed up by Smith, Lawler and Alec Lindsay. In midfield, there's the work-rate of Hughes, Hall and Ian Callaghan — and some subtlety to go with it. And up front, the darting speed of Heighway, not to mention his intelligent play; the lofty Toshack; and the irrepressible Keegan.

Leeds have been around the top for several seasons now—the team they've all had to beat in the chase of honours. They will be there again next time out. Derby have emerged as a force, and seem certain to contest the honours again, although they may lack strength in depth. Manchester City, Manchester United; the London clubs — Arsenal, Chelsea and Spurs. These will all be ambitious to make their mark when kick-off time comes around.

But after Liverpool's run to Wembley, followed by their surge through to join the championship

pacemakers at the end of last season, everyone will look at Bill Shankly's Reds with renewed respect—and not a little fear—as "term time" looms again. And, if Liverpool DO carry on where they left off, other managers are going to frame the question (if only to themselves): WILL LIVERPOOL EMERGE AS THE TEAM OF THE SEVENTIES?

It's a question to which we could well see the start of the answer in the coming months. And if Liverpool find the honours falling thick and fast into their lap, as happened during the 1960s, Bill Shankly will be as proud as punch. As he always is of Liverpool—of course.

Shankly stories are numerous, and some of them are legend. But one which is true—it happened to me, so I know it to be fact—just about sums up the feeling Bill has for Liverpool. He doesn't like anyone to sell them short, even minutely, and even unintentionally.

I had written a piece about Liverpool, and their glory years of the 1960s. Their emergence from the Second Division, and those stunning successes of League title, F.A. Cup and League title again, in a devastating hat-trick.

I met Bill at a Tranmere Rovers game shortly afterwards. "That was a guid article you did," he said. And then, just as I was about to glow at the compliment, he added gravely: *"But you missed out one thing— we won the F.A. Charity Shield, as well."*

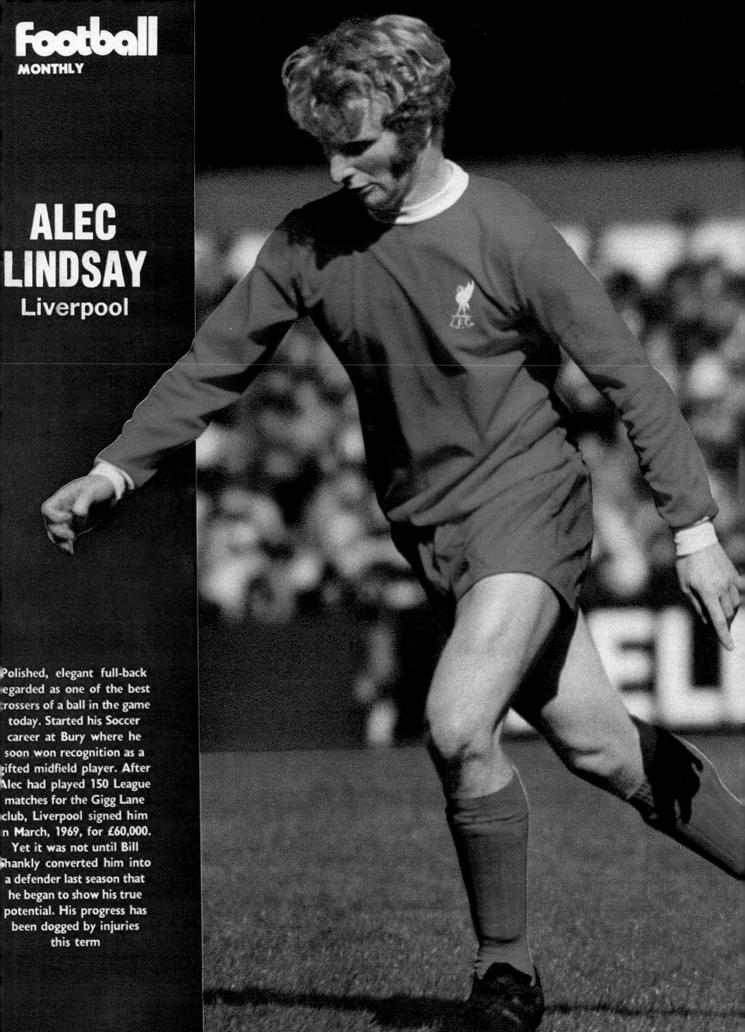

Football
MONTHLY

ALEC LINDSAY
Liverpool

Polished, elegant full-back regarded as one of the best crossers of a ball in the game today. Started his Soccer career at Bury where he soon won recognition as a gifted midfield player. After Alec had played 150 League matches for the Gigg Lane club, Liverpool signed him in March, 1969, for £60,000. Yet it was not until Bill Shankly converted him into a defender last season that he began to show his true potential. His progress has been dogged by injuries this term

Football MONTHLY

LIVERPOOL

Football League Champions in 1901, 1906, 1922, 1923, 1947, 1964 and 1966. F.A. Cup Winners in 1965. That's the impressive total of honours behind the Merseyside club.

Manager Bill Shankly has patiently re-built a new Liverpool into one of the most powerful and combative squads in the First Division. But then that's the way we have always come to regard the men who wear the famous red shirt with pride.

With such strength-in-depth and the will-to-win that characterises all Shankly's sides, Liverpool will be there or thereabouts in the season's final reckoning . . . as usual!

Here is the proud Anfield line-up.

Back row (left to right): John McLaughlin, Phil Boersma, Phil Thomson, Trevor Storton, Alex Lindsay, Peter Cormack, Kevin Keegan.

Middle: Jack Whitham, Larry Lloyd, Frank Lane, Ray Clemence, John Toshack, Steve Heighway.

Front: Ian Callaghan, Emlyn Hughes, Peter Thompson, Tommy Smith, Brian Hall and Chris Lawler.

❝I'M A TOUGH GUY—

says Tommy Smith

Football

FOUNDED IN 1951 BY CHARLES BUCHAN
CAPTAIN OF SUNDERLAND,
ARSENAL AND ENGLAND

FEBRUARY, 1973
No. 258

EDITOR: **PAT COLLINS**
ART EDITOR: **REGINALD BASS**
PHOTOGRAPHER: **IAN McLENNAN**
ADVERTISEMENT MANAGER: **G. A. IRELAND**

Tommy Smith in a mean and determined mood as he is challenged by Colin Bell of Manchester City. In the background is Chris Lawler, a close friend who joined the Anfield groundstaff at the same time as Smith

◀◀ November 1972 | ▲ February 1973

AND PROUD OF IT!

THEY say I'm the hardest man in football, but there's no truth in the rumour that my studs are screwed straight into my feet. They couldn't penetrate my skin anyway!

But seriously, I'm proud of my reputation as a tough guy. That's the way I like to play the game—hard but always fair, 50-50 tackling and no other nonsense. Since I was a youngster I've had to live with this rough and tough image. When I left school at 14 I was 5 ft. 8 in. and weighed 11½ stone. I was always a big lad!

Let me say right now that I have never deliberately set out to injure a player, that's not me at all. I'd pack up the game altogether if that ever happened. It's a man's game, but I want no part of anything vicious.

My reputation seems to worry a lot of players and when they are more conscious of you than the actual game they cannot be doing their jobs properly. Perhaps I'm being a little conceited when I say that some strikers don't want to know when I'm around.

That's their fault . . . I never shy away from a tackle and when I go in I give it everything I've got. My job is to win the ball and I reckon I'm fairly useful at doing just that. At least, I don't seem to get a lot of arguments with that opinion!

One player I really admire is Chelsea's Ian Hutchinson and I felt excited for him when he returned to action just before Christmas in such a convincing manner. He has been one of the game's unluckiest players with the injuries he has had to endure over the past two years.

You could be sure when you played opposite Ian that he'd really give you a game to remember. I've seen him dive into crowded goalmouths where I would have second thoughts. With his tremendous courage he makes sure he gives as much as he takes. *What I like about him most is that he's not a moaner.*

I've tackled players who roll over in a real dying swan act. They are the first to rush to the referee and complain. "Hutch" accepts the rough side of the game and gets on with the business of scoring goals—which he does very well. He's a thoroughbred professional.

It riles me sometimes when critics accuse me of lacking sufficient skills. Mostly it goes in one ear and out the other. I'll start to worry when they can't find the words to spill out about me!

But I'd just like to say that no player in the world could succeed in the First Division without a certain amount of ability and as I've been around on the scene for the past ten years. I think my record speaks for itself.

With my particular style it's surprising that I've had very few bad injuries from my time in football. Being a tough tackler, it is essential that you don't go in halfhearted as that can be a big danger to a player. You must have the determination to go right through with the job and I believe this has helped me steer clear of injuries.

Strangely enough, the only two serious injuries I've had came against Continental opposition. Two years ago Liverpool were playing Vitoria Setubal in Portugal when I challenged one of their little forwards. He went completely over the top and took a big chunk of my kneecap with him.

Last season a player from Servette took a wild swing and I ended up with a six-inch gap from my ankle to my shin.

But these incidents apart I've been fairly lucky. Although just before Christmas I was unfortunate with an injury that had nothing to do with football.

I was driving to my home in Ormskirk when my car skidded into the banking and I spent two weeks in hospital with broken ribs. Still, it could have been much worse and I was back training in next to no time.

Over the past two seasons a tremendous amount of publicity has been given to the new stricter interpretation of the laws by our Football League referees. I fully realise that the amount of petulance and spite in the game was threatening to destroy it as a spectacle, but I believe they have gone from one extreme to the other.

Of course, the game needed cleaning-up, but not to the extent of players being booked for any trivial offence. I have already gone on record as saying that football is developing into a "softtouch." I still firmly believe

that's the way it's heading. *Ask yourself this question: Would the public go to see a match in which all the physical contact—the lifeblood of Soccer —has been eliminated?*

I will admit that one aspect of the campaign, that of getting rid of the tackle from behind, is beneficial. That has been for the good of the game in general.

But the trouble, I believe, stems from the fact that we have amateur officials controlling 22 professional men who rely on football for their livelihood.

Referees have a tough job and I have a lot of sympathy and respect for the way they go about it. But in reality the bad ones outnumber the good ones.

Control is far too inconsistent. I've played in matches where a player has been booked for nothing more than a tackle that has been mistimed—and you get that kind of incident in every single match, believe me. In others deliberate fouling has passed unpunished. These are the situations that referees have got to come to terms with. Little wonder they get so much stick!

I honestly believe the answer lies in full-time professional referees who have the time and place to study the game inside out and realise the difference between

an unlucky tackle and a blatant foul.

This job would be ideal for players when they have hung up their boots at around 35. They could get really involved with the playing side of football, visit clubs and get that little bit closer to the players. And we could all understand their difficulties as well.

As it stands now referees have little contact with the game except for a period of 90 minutes on a Saturday afternoon where his handling of situations is vital. It's not the kind of job that I would like in the circumstances.

As skipper of a fine Liverpool side it is my job to see that things run smoothly on the field and manager Bill Shankly has drummed into all of us that it is pointless arguing with the referee once a decision has been given.

Which brings me on to Bill, who has done a marvellous job in re-fashioning the team so quickly after the club's brilliant success of the Sixties.

Everyone has a favourite Bill Shankly story, he is such a fabulous character. Being associated with him since I joined the Anfield groundstaff at 15, I have witnessed many hilarious incidents that have had us all in stitches. When you live and work with someone like Shanks you tend to accept his humour

The famous Bill Shankly . . . "When you live and work with him you tend to accept his humour as part of the normal way of life at Anfield," says Tommy

as part of the normal way of life at Anfield!

He is famous for standing by our dressing-room door when the opposition turn up and as they walk in he'll turn around and state in all seriousness: "No trouble lads, they all look as if they've had a few pints on the way here. And that centre half! He looks as if he's been up all night."

Whenever he talks about his own playing career he always reminds us of the day when he knew it was time to quit . . . when he had to go on to the terraces to retrieve the ball himself while playing for Preston at Deepdale!

Just when everyone is thinking of a lovely afternoon off, Bill will suddenly call a team-meeting at three o'clock in the afternoon. Does he discuss tactics for the following match? Not likely. He'll talk about what will be on the menu at the hotel or the sleeping arrangements. More often than not we will end up by talking about one of the big games like Wales v. England!

What does get his back up is when we are trailing at Anfield. He'll walk into the dressing-room at half-time with a grim face and pound the floor for a while. Then he starts: "There are 50,000 fans out there and 49,500 are for you. You've let them all down. We can't let it happen to these people."

That's Shanks. Despite his Scottish ancestry he is a Scouse through and through. The lads on the terraces are his people. They're the only ones he really wants to know.

Some of the funniest stories have occurred abroad. Like when we were playing in Romania and he had a set-to with a waiter at our hotel.

A few of the lads asked for a Coke one afternoon and were told there was none available although we had seen some in the kitchen. Bill saw red, leapt out of his chair and marched into the kitchen from which he emerged with a crate of the stuff and handed them around.

He went on to give this waiter the worst-ticking off I've ever heard. He told him he would be writing to the Kremlin and demand that the unfortunate fellow be carted off to the salt-mines in Siberia!

The hotel staff were as good as gold to us all after that!

Another time, playing in a summer tournament in the States, we were due to meet a German side in the final. Bill discovered that their team preferred to play with a soft ball and told us to watch out for their tricks.

He was standing on the touchline giving some last-minute instructions when he saw the keeper pick up the match ball with his back turned.

That was enough for Bill. He dashed on the pitch, grabbed the ball from the keeper and threatened to knock his block off. The only trouble was that the German was about 6 ft. 4 in. tall, broad as a barn door and weighed around 16 stone! The crowd were in hysterics.

In a similar tournament in New York he was sitting quietly in the stand watching a match. A big, loud-mouthed spectator was a nuisance by shouting at the players throughout the game, Bill's temper was reaching boiling point when the spectator dropped his glasses. Shanks quickly saw the chance to shut him up. He trod on the glasses, then flicked them aside.

We never heard a squeak from him—Bill even had the cheek to say how sorry he was!

All this does not disguise his real abilities as a manager —you don't need me to remind you just what he has achieved in his years at Anfield. What the lads respect most is the tremendous enthusiasm which continually inspires us. He is as fit and rarin' to go as ever and still puts a few of us in our place during training.

Above all, he has the knack of being able to turn little-known players into world-beaters and his shrewdness in the transfer market is

reflected in the likes of Kevin Keegan, Steve Heighway, Ray Clemence and Larry Lloyd who were all picked up at bargain prices.

I was born in the famous Scotland Road district of Liverpool so it was only natural that I should be a devoted Reds' fan as a youngster. But it was only the unfortunate death of my father when I was 15 that prompted me into becoming a professional footballer.

Would you believe that Tommy Smith's original ambition was to become an architect?

I was attending college and receiving a grant of £52 a year to help in my studies when my father caught pneumonia and died. It meant that I had to become the bread-winner for the family and Liverpool's £8-a-week offer to join the groundstaff was an opportunity that couldn't be turned down. Even now I can remember the day my mother took me along to Anfield and asked Mr. Shankly to take care of me.

I have never regretted the decision for Soccer has enabled me to see the world and provided some outstanding experiences. For the first two years of my apprenticeship I was nothing more than a labourer and as I was the biggest lad of the bunch I was given all the arduous jobs, like climbing and painting the floodlights for example. Chris Lawler was signed up at the same time and we struck up an immediate friendship.

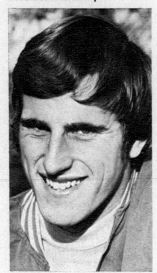

RAY CLEMENCE . . .
one of Shankly's bargain discoveries

All the time I was gaining experience and was soon put into the Central League side, playing against men. So I learned from an early age to be able to stand up and look after myself, most necessary in such an atmosphere.

Eventually I made a First Division place my own—in time to share the glory of the club's first FA Cup Final success in 1965, followed by the League Championship of 1966.

The highlight of my career so far is that Cup win over Leeds United at Wembley when Ian St. John's brilliant diving header clinched the game in extra-time.

The scenes on our journey back to Liverpool were unbelievable. The fans were going mad, they had lined up for miles outside the city.

Normally it would take ten minutes to drive from Lime Street to the Town Hall, but in our open-topped bus it took TWO HOURS!

I've never seen so many people. They hung from windows and any possible vantage point. It was one of the few times I've ever really been moved to tears.

The next time Liverpool appeared at Wembley, against Arsenal in 1971, only Ian Callaghan, Chris Lawler, Peter Thompson and myself were left of the '65 side. But it was not our day and the Gunners snatched victory in extra-time. It was still a magnificent achievement in reaching the Final when you consider the club were in a period of transition.

Since then our young players have matured and blossomed into a superbly drilled outfit. Frankly, it comes as no real shock to ourselves that we are sitting on top of the First Division. We KNOW we are a good side—you don't beat a team like Leeds twice on their own patch if you're not!

There is not a weakness in any department. We have strength at the back, skill and power in the middle of the park and the essential flair in attack that can conjure goals from nothing.

Moreover, we have the kind of super-fitness that enables us to finish a game as strongly as we start it.

With such a perfectly equipped young side we're all confident that the future holds many exciting happenings for the 'Pool.

Like the club's eighth League Championship success come May.

May 1973 ▶

Nice big smiles all round from Tommy Smith's family,
pictured at their home in Ormskirk, just outside Liverpool.
The pretty little girl on Dad's lap is Janette (5) and
that cheekie chappie sitting in front of Mum (Sue) is Darren (7).

STEVE
HEIGHWAY
Liverpool

Football
MONTHLY

▲ December 1972

BRIAN HALL
LIVERPOOL

'There's nothing to touch the Anfield spirit'

EMLYN HUGHES

He's the perfect Liverpool type

by KEITH FISHER

EMLYN HUGHES emerged from Liverpool's eighth League Championship success last season to confirm the belief that the club possess the most complete all-round footballer in the business.

And if you had to choose one individual who best personifies all the grittiness and fighting qualities of Bill Shankly's formidable Red Army then Hughes would be the natural candidate.

This Anfield powerhouse combines his sturdy defensive duties in midfield with a ceaseless energy that enables him to score vital goals following direct and penetrative runs from deep in his own area. There are few more tingling sights than Hughes in vigorous flight ready to unleash one of his right-foot specials.

Son of a Welshman who played Rugby League for Barrow, Emlyn was Lot No. I in Shankly's rebuilding plans after age had finally crept up on his great side of the early Sixties. The £65,000 fee which was handed over to Blackpool in February, 1967, must go down as even one of Shank's biggest bargains.

No player worked harder to help land the title. His contribution in terms of effort and enterprise proved a decisive influence as the club brushed aside the persistence of Arsenal and Leeds. Modest and unassuming, he scorns the spotlight and points to the success of the fellows around him.

Says Hughes: "We came through in the end because everyone was prepared to run until they dropped. That's how much it meant to us. It was the culmination of two years' bloody hard slog.

"It's impossible to pick out someone for particular mention. You hear players talking about the great team-spirit at their clubs, but I doubt if anything can touch what we have here.

"The boss has drummed into us the need to do things collectively, as one compact unit, and that's why Liverpool will never have to rely on one individual to do the work for us. Sure, we have players like Kevin Keegan and Steve Heighway who are encouraged to do their own thing, but it is within the framework of the team as a whole.

"Take last season's goals and you'll find that nearly everyone got his name on the scoring list. We are all willing to work and chase for each other. It doesn't matter who puts the ball in the back of the net, just as long as it gets there.

"Playing for a club like Liverpool is a bit special, anyway. It sounds corny, but when you slip on that red jersey it seems to carry you around the field on its own.

"Then there's Shanks who never lets you forget what a privilege it is to be at Anfield! You get the feeling that he'll gladly swop positions for the chance to score in front of the Kop."

It is the extrovert Shankly who receives the biggest tribute from Hughes for the Championship triumph.

"You've got to hand it to the man when you consider his record since he came here," he says. "His greatness lies in the fact that he watched one great side fall apart, then went out and built another. He inspires you with an infectious optimism that makes you sit up straight and listen.

"There's never a dull moment when he's around, although when you live and work with him all the time you tend to take his humour more or less for granted. He honestly believes no team has a right to be on the same pitch as Liverpool.

"He just cannot understand if we lose. After a match in which we've played terrible he'll come down and say, 'It's not your fault, lads. They had unbelievable luck and that keeper—he'll never play another game like that in his life!' What can you say?

"When we practically clinched the League by beating Leeds 2-0 at Anfield on Easter Monday he was near to tears. It's typical of the man that, when he walked on to the field to salute the

football

JULY, 1973
No. 263

FOUNDED IN 1951 BY CHARLES BUCHAN
CAPTAIN OF SUNDERLAND,
ARSENAL AND ENGLAND

EDITOR: **PAT COLLINS**
ART EDITOR: **REGINALD BASS**
PHOTOGRAPHER: **IAN McLENNAN**
ADVERTISEMENT MANAGER: **G. A. IRELAND**

▲ July 1973

Kop, he took off his jacket to reveal a red shirt. They lapped it up. He's really a Scouse through and through.

"He played an important part in that victory. Before the game we were sitting down in the dressing-room and hardly a word was spoken because we were so nervous. It was a match we had to win.

"Then Shanks arrived with half-an-hour to go. 'Nothing to worry about today,' he said casually. 'I've just seen the Leeds boys. They look white with fright.' Incredible isn't he?"

A close scrutiny of Liverpool's statistics over the past two years reveals the sort of super-consistency which, Leeds apart, has earned envious admiration from the rest of the First Division.

They served notice of the title intentions in 1972, when they finished third after a tremendous late run-in of 17 matches which included only one defeat, and that at the hands of eventual champions Derby County.

The momentum of that rousing finale carried over to last season, although it is a sore point with Hughes that some critics carp over their supposed lack of subtlety and craft.

He adds: "We are used to it by now and the more you keep winning the more you seem to come under fire. It doesn't worry us, we just let our points total do the talking for us. Even so, when you consider we have exciting players like Keegan and Heighway it's something

EMLYN HUGHES

that's hard to understand.

"When I first joined the club I was bemused by it all. No matter where we played everyone raised their game to such an extent that they played like world-beaters just to put one over on Liverpool.

"We must be the original team everyone loves to see beaten. That we have managed to maintain our consistency is surely a tribute to the never-say-die character in the side.

"There can't be many who would deny our right to the title. We have proved to be the best and most consistent side in the Football League.

"We played Leeds four times last season, won three and drew the other. There are teams in the First Division who haven't managed to do it once in years! That speaks for itself."

Hughes highlights the problems facing our top players when he reflects ruefully on the strains and stresses that have to be endured over an arduous campaign. "The pressure on the modern footballer can be unbearable at times," he says.

"I'll be honest and admit that towards the end I was all in and was running around on instinct.

"People go on about the lack of skill in the game, but with such a tough schedule to keep it's impossible to get the priorities right. That's why a lot of the stuff these days is purely physical. Everything revolves around fitness and it's got to be that way to survive.

"The energy which has been my biggest asset deserted me at the death. Luckily, being part of a successful organization helps pull you through. But imagine playing over 70 games and ending up with nothing.

"I was glad when it was all over. The pressures built up after every match we won. We were always top of the table from almost the first kick and were always there to be caught. The lads could never relax.

"The emotional strain of the last month was agonizing.

The championship was there for the taking, so long as we kept our heads. I felt confident we'd do it, but there are so many nagging suspicions that drive you up the wall.

"I must have been hell to live with. I'd get home from training and start working out goal averages!

"On top of all that my wife Barbara was expecting our first baby and things couldn't have been very pleasant for her. Mind you, when you get your hands on that trophy at the end of all your hard work you'd go through it again!"

He advocates a pruning-down of the number of clubs in the First Division as the answer. "If we had 18 teams life would be so much easier," he says.

"There would be more time for planning and preparation and everything need not be done in a mad rush. Another thing is that the public is saturated with football. There would be an immediate improvement in the overall standard."

His impressive displays for England have been a heartening feature for Sir Alf Ramsey. The muscular Hughes has developed into a key player at full-back, after taking over from Terry Cooper, and with his permanency has come polish and assurance.

He is caught between two stools. Although he started League life as a defender with Blackpool, soon after his switch to Merseyside he was thrust into a midfield role. Despite the occasional reversion to his former position, it is in the No. 6 jersey that the club have learned to capitalize on his strength and shooting.

So where does his preference lie? "As a professional footballer I'm prepared to play anywhere. It doesn't really worry me where I operate as long as my name is on the team-sheet.

"My natural instinct is to defend and that's where I learned the game. But I like the freedom a player is allowed in midfield, and you can express yourself more fully.

"When I came to Anfield I never imagined I would end up there. The team had a few injuries and the boss picked me against Stoke City. He never discussed it at all and still hasn't done so. It happened and that's where I've stayed!"

Hughes, at 25, has already reached the top of his profession. Yet Shankly can afford a quiet smile, knowing that he has still to reach his peak as a player.

Born in Barrow, he was spotted by a Blackpool scout in local Soccer and packed off to Bloomfield Road, where he was told by manager Ron Suart that he lacked sufficient height to make the grade. Hughes was 16. Suart sent him home, armed with a body-building diet, and instructions to report back in a year.

Hughes duly obliged. By which time he had thickened out. Within six months after his return he had made his debut against Blackburn Rovers. Such was his progress that after only 25 First Division appearances he was snapped up by Shankly and the canny Scot rates it one of the best deals he has made.

Now a strapping figure, standing 5 ft. 10 in. and weighing nearly 12st., Hughes looks back on his early days, with special reference to Suart.

He says: "I was at Bloomfield Road for two-and-a-half years and learned an awful lot. Ronnie is a real gentleman and I left just after he was sacked in 1967. But before he went he called me into his office and told me he would fix me up with a leading club. Within weeks I was packing my bags."

Liverpool are clearly on the crest, but Hughes anticipates a harder time next season. "Everyone will now be trying doubly hard to nail us, but the side has so much character and talent that the future looks exciting.

"Last season gave us the breakthrough we needed after seven barren years, and for Liverpool that's wasted time. It was also my first major honour and I was delighted. Now we're aiming for the European Cup—we'd like to win that one for the boss. But above all we have the confidence to stay at the top for several years."

Steve Heighway adds craft and subtlety to the Liverpool side

Soccer Annual 1972-73

Liverpool manager Bill Shankly takes a long look at the League Championship Trophy his club won. It's a long look that tells of a hard and heavy haul at the top where the Reds led the way for most of the season with all the pressures that went with it

10-PAGE REVIEW

KEVIN KEEGAN says

I THOUGHT BILL SHANKLY WAS KIDDING WHEN HE ASKED . . .

THE GREATEST moment of my Soccer life came early in August last year, just before the start of the season.

I had joined Liverpool from Scunthorpe only three months previously—just a few days before the Reds lost to Arsenal in the Cup Final at Wembley.

Their defeat was as big a disappointment to me, the newcomer, as it was to any of the Anfield old hands. I was determined to do my utmost for my new club, and I longed for a place in the League side.

I knew this wouldn't come easily and when pre-season training started and I saw the size and quality of the staff, I was even more aware that I would have to work like never before to achieve that ambition.

I played in three pre-season friendly games for the Reserves against Tranmere Rovers, Southport and New Brighton and although at Scunthorpe I had always played in midfield with either No. 7 or No. 10 on my back, I scored three goals in those games.

Then came the final practice game at our Melwood training ground—League side v. Reserves, and in these games it is usually the reserves who win.

For this game I was genuinely surprised to be chosen for the League side—and we beat the Reserves 6–0, of which I scored four!

Naturally, I was pleased with myself, but it was still a shock when, a couple of days before our opening game with Nottingham Forest at Anfield, the Boss took me on one side and almost floored me with the question . . .

" *What would you like to do on Saturday—play for the first team—or the reserves?* "

Which would I like . . .? I thought for a moment that he was kidding me along—but I only needed one look at his face to know that Mr. Bill Shankly was deadly serious.

I realised afterwards that no doubt he had every intention of including me in the League side, but being the man he is, he gave *me* the chance to opt out.

This was the furthest thing from my mind for one thing I have never lacked is confidence in my ability.

My reply was perhaps cheeky as I

'LIKE TO PLAY FOR THE FIRST TEAM?'

said quite honestly: " I've come here to play in the First Division." I wasn't going to miss the BIG chance.

But on the day of the match I came mighty near to committing professional suicide, as I set off to drive to the Anfield Road ground.

Having only had previous League experience at Scunthorpe where they didn't exactly get enormous crowds, I started in what I thought was plenty of time. But I failed to take into account the traffic that converges on Anfield for *any* game.

And I got stuck fast in a traffic-jam, arriving a good ten minutes late!

Not the best of starts to a First Division career, I agree, but I didn't let it bother me. What did worry me more than a little was the size of the ground,

and then the feast of noise from the huge crowd when we got out on the pitch.

But I put my every ounce of concentration into the game and was completely over the moon when I scored after only 12 minutes!

I was delighted, not only for myself, but for the Boss. At least I had justified the confidence he had in me. And I have plenty more to thank him for.

Without any doubt he has been the major influence in my being a member of one of the finest teams in the game. But others helped me, too, in my early days.

First there was my father. When it came to a question of a normal job or a possible career in football he didn't try to influence me at all. " It's your life," he said, " you must make your own decision."

Then there was my headmaster at St. Peter's Secondary School at Doncaster. When I was 15, I had a chance to sign as an apprentice with Coventry City, but he and my father persuaded me to stay on at school for a year and take my ' O ' levels.

Leaving school at 16, I took a job as a clerk at a brass foundry, and played football for the works reserve team. I also played for Elmfield House Youth Club and on Sundays for a " pub " team.

In one of these Sunday games I was being marked by one Bob Nellish who only the day previously had been asked by Scunthorpe to keep his eyes open for any promising juniors.

I must have given him a bit of a game for he asked me to go to Scunthorpe. I played in three junior games for them and on New Year's Day 1968 signed apprentice forms.

At the end of that season Scunthorpe were relegated to the Fourth Division, and in the general shake-up for the new season I got the chance to play in midfield, which remained my position until I moved to Liverpool three years later. I had more than a hundred League games for the United, and scored ten goals in my final season.

Whether this last season's record induced Mr. Shankly to give me a chance as a striker I don't know, but that has been my role ever since.

Perhaps my best game so far for

Keegan in aerial action against Bernard Shaw of Wolves at Molineux

Liverpool was the Third Round F.A. Cup-Tie last season against Oxford United when I got two goals in a ten-minute spell, and we beat them 3–0.

It wasn't so much the goals themselves, but the manner in which they were scored. This was one of those games when things went just right.

My best goal yet is probably one that I scored in our 5—0 win against Newcastle United. John Toshack got the ball on the half-way line, and was forced to move back towards our

Liverpool manager **Bill Shankly** (centre) laying the law down to players (from left to right) **Larry Lloyd, John Toshack, Alec Lindsay, Tommy Smith** and **Brian Hall**.
Below: Welsh international **John Toshack** in action.

defence. I ran forward, took the ball from him, continued running, and was faced by Bobby Moncur, who back-pedalled. Then I dummied him and another approaching defender—and cracked the ball home from about 25 yards out.

You've no idea of the feeling when a shot like that comes off. It went in like a rocket before the goalkeeper could even move. And that after running from the half-way line! I was chuffed, I can tell you.

I've scored my share of lucky goals too, none luckier than an occasion when I was playing for Scunthorpe against Oldham. We were attacking down the left, and I was just right of centre when the ball came over.

Three big defenders jumped for it, and the next thing I knew was that they had all missed. It hit me smack on the forehead and flashed into the net for what proved to be the winning goal!

But apart from the thrill of first being selected for the Liverpool side our tremendous run at the end of last season made me proud to be a member of such a team and such a club.

And when I say "team" I mean everyone concerned with the Liverpool Football Club. We have no passengers . . .

Liverpool *is* a team . . .

Meet the STARS

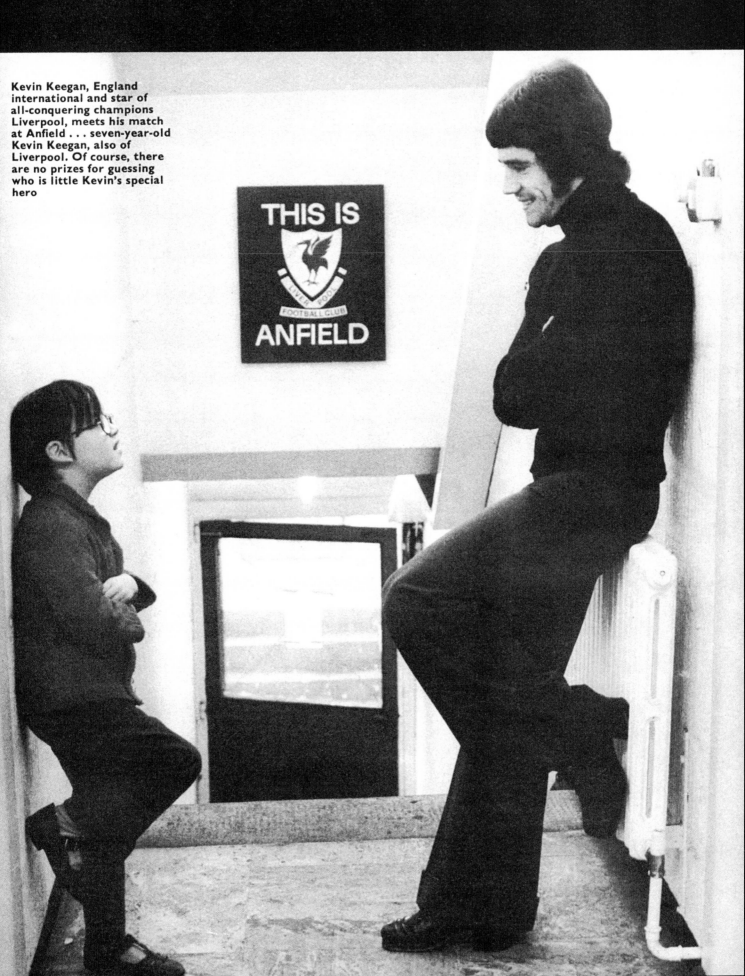

Kevin Keegan, England international and star of all-conquering champions Liverpool, meets his match at Anfield . . . seven-year-old Kevin Keegan, also of Liverpool. Of course, there are no prizes for guessing who is little Kevin's special hero

THIS IS
ANFIELD

Postscript

The average playing career of today's professional footballer rarely exceeds fifteen years, but during those years he may, if sufficiently talented, astute and lucky, earn enough not to have to worry about his financial prospects ever again.

Not so the generation of players featured in *Football Monthly*.

Before the abolition of the £20 a week maximum wage in 1961 footballers earned little more than the average working man. After 1961, some individuals did extremely well. But still it was never sufficient to buy a lifetime's security.

Then there were the mental torments; the pain of adjusting to the mundanities of life after the final whistle had blown.

Almost as soon as he resigned in 1974, Bill Shankly regretted his haste and took to hanging around the Melwood training ground until even his old pal Bob Paisley had to beg him to stay away.

Shankly revealed his inner torment in public only once. But the occasion would lead to what has become one of the most oft repeated, yet most widely misunderstood football quotes of all time.

In 1976, both Shankly and Harold Wilson (who had himself just resigned as Prime Minister at the comparatively young age of 60) were interviewed by Shelley Rhodie on Granada TV's *Live from Two* programme.

In contemplative mood, Shankly said, 'Everything I've got, I owe to football. You only get out of the game what you put into it, Shelley. And I put everything into it that I could, and still do, for the people, and for the people I was playing for, and the people I was manager for.

'Everything,' Shankly repeated. 'I didn't cheat them out of anything. So I've put my heart and soul, to the extent that my family suffered.'

Sensing a vulnerability in the usually brittle Shankly, Rhodie asked, 'Do you regret that at all?'

Shankly responded, 'Yes! Oh I regret it very much! Yes.'

And then he paused, and added in a rush, 'Some may say that "Football's a matter of life and death to you", and I'd say "Listen, I'd be disappointed with that; it's more important than that". And that's true.'

At which point Harold Wilson cut in, 'Yes, it's a religion.'

Shankly agreed. 'It's a religion... and my family suffered. They've been neglected.'

Now the interview took an unexpectedly dark turn. Rhodie asked, 'How would you do it now, if you had your time again?'

Shankly now seemed unsure, perhaps even bashful that he had revealed a more tender side.

'I don't know really,' he said slowly, but without conviction. 'If I had the same thoughts, possibly I'd do the same thing again...'

Hardly the words of a man who felt that football was indeed more important than life and death.

In complete contrast, Billy Liddell always made it quite clear that football satisfied only a part of his ambitions. Having worked as an accountant throughout his playing career, after his final game in August 1960 he was appointed Bursar for Liverpool University. Forever active in community affairs, he also served as president of the Liverpool Supporters Club and as chairman of Littlewoods' *Spot the Ball* panel. He died from Alzheimer's in 2001, aged 79 and is remembered by a plaque at Anfield. Those who recall him speak of him in almost saintly terms.

Of Liddell's team-mates, many followed the well-trodden path into coaching, scouting or management.

Tommy Younger became a scout for Leeds United, before coaching in Canada. He later found success as a businessman and at the time of his premature death, aged 53, in 1984, was chairman of Hibernian.

Jimmy Melia, after continuing his playing career at Wolves and Southampton, enjoyed a remarkably varied career, commencing as player-manager with Aldershot and Crewe, followed by Southport and Brighton, whom he led to the 1983 FA Cup final (coincidentally via a shock 5th Round win at Anfield). Thereafter he spent three years at Belenenses of Portugal, before setting up a football academy in the United Arab Emirates. His most recent port of call was the USA, where he coaches at the Dallas Texans Soccer Club.

Another great traveller has been Gordon Milne. After leaving Liverpool for Blackpool in 1967, he joined Wigan Athletic, then a non-League club, as player-manager in 1970, became part-time England Youth team manager in 1972, then after taking over at Coventry in 1974 was considered for the full England manager's job. His later clubs included Leicester, the Turkish club Besiktas, where he won three league titles in succession between 1990–92, then Nagoya Grampus 8 in Japan in 1994, before returning to Istanbul for a further spell at Fenerbahce. Back in England he was then appointed Chief Executive of the League Managers' Association before accepting the role as Director of Football at Newcastle, followed in 2005 by an advisory role at his previous club, Besiktas. He finally retired in 2006.

Incidentally, his one year old son Andrew (*see page 50*) did follow in his father's footsteps, not as a footballer, but as an apprentice carpenter (Gordon's first job), and is still in the building trade today.

Of the later generation of players to turn to management, the two most prominent have been John Toshack and Kevin Keegan, who as joint strikers for Liverpool during the 1970s were said to have shared a telepathic understanding (a claim tested in a televised test, with inconclusive but intriguing results).

Awarded an OBE for managing Swansea's amazing rise from the Fourth to the First Division in three successive seasons (and not for his infamous book of poetry, *Gosh It's Tosh*), Toshack has managed in Spain (for Real Madrid, Real Sociedad, Deportivo La Coruna and Real Murcia), France (St Etienne), Turkey (Besiktas) and Italy (Catania). His latest post is as manager of Wales, where his assistant is his former team-mate and Anfield boss, Roy Evans.

Keegan, meanwhile, also an OBE, has barely left the headlines since leaving Anfield in 1977 for Hamburg. After finishing his playing career at Newcastle in 1984 he returned to St James' Park as manager in 1992, and again in 2008, with spells in between as manager of Fulham, England and Manchester City. As to seven year old Kevin Keegan we encountered on page 139, he still lives in Liverpool but is no longer a fan.

One of the abiding characteristics of Liverpool is the so-called 'Liverpool Way,' referring to the number of former players who stay on in one role or another, as was true of Phil Taylor, Bob Paisley, Ronnie Moran, Roy Evans and, in later generations, Kenny Dalglish and Graeme Souness.

Geoff Twentyman, for example, enjoyed a second career at Liverpool that outdid anything he achieved on the pitch. Invited back by Shankly in 1967 to become Chief Scout, Twentyman is credited with spotting such talents as Phil Neal, Alan Hansen, Kenny Dalglish and Ian Rush. In 1986 he moved to a similar position at Rangers. He died in Southport in 2004, aged 74.

Where does a player go after Anfield? The short answer seems to be across the Mersey to Tranmere. Willie Stevenson (*right*) ended his League career there after a five year interlude at Stoke, and later ran a cleaning company in Macclesfield. Bobby Graham (*far right*) who signed for Liverpool eight months after his fellow Motherwellian Ian St John, followed the Saint both to Coventry and Tranmere, and again to Motherwell when St John was manager there in the mid 1970s.

His replacement as Chief Scout was Ron Yeats. After finishing his playing career across the water at Tranmere, Yeats managed Rovers for a spell, had a season in North American soccer, but then returned to scout for Liverpool. He retired in 2006 but is still a popular figure on the Anfield scene.

Yeats admitted that management just did not suit his temperament. The same was true of Chris Lawler. After finishing his career at Portsmouth and Stockport he joined the Anfield coaching staff and trained the reserves. However, he soon gave up. Football management, he said, seemed to bring out the worst in people. Thereafter he coached youngsters in the Merseyside area.

Both Liverpool's graduate players, Brian Hall and Steve Heighway, found second careers at Anfield.

Hall, who later played for Plymouth and Burnley, has acted as Liverpool's Public Relations Executive since 1991, overseeing the club's work with charities and community groups, as well as looking after match day competitions and events.

After coaching in the USA, Steve Heighway was appointed Director of the Liverpool Academy in 1989, a role he kept until 2007. During this time he worked with a succession of starlets, Michael Owen and Steven Gerrard included, winning three FA Youth Cups in the process. He now works as an ambassador for the club, with special responsbility for a proposed Liverpool Academy in the USA.

Just as Charles Buchan himself made the transition from playing to reporting, three former Liverpool players featured would go on to prominent roles in the media.

With Jimmy Greaves, Ian St John co-presented ITV's long-running *Saint and Greavsie* Saturday show, which ran from 1985–92.

Thereafter the 'Saint' continued to appear on television and radio. Still popular on the after-dinner circuit, since the 1980s he has also organised numerous Ian St John Soccer Camps around Britain.

Emlyn 'Crazy Horse' Hughes achieved a similar media profile. After two years in management with Rotherham, in 1984 he was chosen as a team captain on BBC TV's *Question of Sport*, playing opposite the former rugby international Bill Beaumont and being constantly ribbed for his high pitched voice and wild enthusiasm. During his three years on the programme he famously hugged one of the guests, Princess Anne, causing a minor uproar, but clearly no real offence, for he later teamed up with her again on the rather less successful *It's a Royal Knockout*.

In addition to commentary work for the BBC, including coverage of the Heysel disaster in 1985, Hughes was immortalised by being 'signed' to the comic book heroes, Melchester Rovers, as part of *Roy of the Rovers*' team.

Immensely popular with the general public, 'Crazy Horse' died from a brain tumour in 2004, aged only 57.

Centre half Larry Lloyd, who went on to achieve great success with Nottingham Forest as a player, also had a spell in the media, as an outspoken radio pundit for Nottingham's Century 106 station. He later retired to Spain.

But for every Heighway or Keegan, St John or Hughes who stayed within the game or in the limelight, dozens would depart to more mundane areas of life.

A common route was to become a publican or shopkeeper.

Alec Lindsay, for example, runs a pub, and by all accounts has no interest in football. Tommy Smith also tried his hand as a publican in Billinge after his playing career

ended under John Toshack at Swansea in 1979. But in common with so many former players of his time, the rigours of two decades of tough defending, countless knocks and pain-killing injections took their toll on his body, and he ended up on disability benefit after hip, knee and elbow replacements. Despite all this and a major heart attack he was still attending matches at Anfield in 2008 and writing a column in the *Liverpool Echo*.

Peter Thompson, after leaving Anfield in 1973, had four years at Bolton, then ran a petrol station near Anfield before becoming a hotelier in Cumbria. He subsequently retired to Portugal.

Geoff Strong and Ian Callaghan co-own a pub, although Strong also runs a hotel furnishing company in Coventry, while Callaghan set up an insurance company in Lydiate, and in recent years has been a mainstay of the Former Players' Association.

After ending his illustrious goal-scoring career at Bolton in 1971, Roger Hunt went back to his family's road haulage business, Hunt Brothers. The company trucks are still a familiar sight in the Merseyside and Cheshire area. Although never actually knighted, 'Sir Roger' did receive an MBE in 2000, and sits on the Pools Panel every Saturday afternoon.

Teenage star Alun Evans played out his career at Aston Villa and Walsall, but ended up delivering bread in Australia. Later he worked as a painter and decorator, while excelling as a veteran cricketer for the Lancashire Over 50's side. His daughter Abby worked for a spell at Anfield, in the Museum and Stadium Tour department.

From the earlier generation, Tommy Leishman worked as a tanker driver for BP Petrol. Jimmy Harrower, who died in 2006, worked as a plasterer. Dave Hickson became a bookmaker, and is now

back at his first club Everton, working as a part-time tour guide.

Dick White ran a garage in Nottingham. Jimmy Payne and Ray Lambert became newsagents, as did Alan A'Court, who had a shop near Bebington. Antonio Rowley set up a printing company in Liverpool, while John Molyneux established a sports equipment business.

Tommy Lawrence, another Red who finished his playing career at Tranmere, in 1973, worked as a quality controller at the same wire factory where he had started as a lad. He has since retired.

Of the whereabouts or fates of the others featured in the Buchan archive, little is known. Kevin Lewis was last heard of in South Africa. Louis Bimpson retired to Burscough. John Evans moved to Essex, Roy Saunders to Swansea, and John McLaughlin has remained in Liverpool.

As for the man whose passion and ego dominated this period like a colossus, Bill Shankly, he died from a heart attack in 1981. Such was his standing that delegates at the Labour Party conference in Brighton observed a minute's silence in respect.

Then in 1997 a statue in his honour was erected outside the Kop, with the inscription, 'He made the people happy'.

There are also gates at Anfield dedicated to him, and to his successor, Bob Paisley.

Liverpudlians are often accused by outsiders of over-sentimentalism. But at Anfield, within its corridors, in its hugely popular club museum, and within the wider archives of British football as a whole, there is good reason for such sentiment.

These men dedicated the best years of their life to the people's game. None of it as important as life itself, for sure, but a wondrous part of life all the same, and of our heritage as a football nation.

Index

Further reading

A'Court, Alan with Hargreaves, Ian *My Life in Football* Bluecoat Press (2003)
Anderson, Jeff and Done, Stephen *The Official Liverpool FC Illustrated History* Carlton (2004)
Anderson, Jeff and Done, Stephen *The Official Liverpool FC Illustrated Encyclopedia* Carlton (2003)
Bowler, Dave *Shanks: The Authorised Biography of Bill Shankly* Orion (1996)
Darby, Tom *Talking Shankly: The Man, the Genius, the Legend* Mainstream (2001)
Doig, Eric *The Essential History of Liverpool* Headline (2003)
Gibson, John *Kevin Keegan – Portrait of a Superstar* WH Allen (1984)
Gill, Karen and Rogers, Ken *The Real Bill Shankly* Trinity Mirror (2007)
Hale, Steve and Thompson, Phil *The Shankly Years – A Revolution in Football* Ebury Press (1998)
Hale, Steve and Ponting, Ivan with Small, Steve *Liverpool in Europe* Carlton (2001)
Hughes, Emlyn *Crazy Horse* Arthur Barker (1980)
Hunt, Roger *Hunt for Goals* Pelham (1969)
Keegan, Kevin *Kevin Keegan* Magnum (1978)
Keegan, Kevin *My Autobiography: Kevin Keegan* Time Warner (1998)
Keith, John *Billy Liddell: The Legend Who Carried the Kop* Robson (2005)
Keith, John *Shanks for the Memory* Robson (2001)
Keith, John *Cally – A Football Phenomenon* Duckworth (1974)
Kelly, Stephen F *Bill Shankly: It's Much More Important Than That* Virgin (1996)
Kelly, Stephen F *Mr Shankly's Photograph* Robson Books (2002)
Liddell, Billy *My Soccer Story* Soccer Book Club (1960)
Lloyd, Larry *Hard Man, Hard Game* John Blake (2008)
Ponting, Ivan and Hale, Steve *The Boot Room – an Anfield Legend* Bluecoat Press (1997)
Ponting, Ivan *Liverpool Player by Player* Bluecoat Press (2006)
Platt, Mark *Cup Kings – Liverpool 1965* Bluecoat Press (2000)
Ridley, Ian *Kevin Keegan: An Intimate Portrait of Football's Last Romantic* Simon & Schuster (2008)
Roberts, John *Bill Shankly: The Forgotten Shankly Tapes* Trinity Mirror (2007)
St John, Ian *Room at the Kop* Pelham (1966)
St John, Ian *The Saint – My Autobiography* Hodder (2006)
Shankly, Bill *Shankly* Arthur Barker (1976)
Smith, Tommy *The Anfield Iron* Bantam Press (2008)
Smith, Tommy *I Did it the Hard Way* Arthur Barker (1980)
Thompson, Phil *Emlyn Hughes: A Tribute to the Crazy Horse* NPI Media (2006)
Thompson, Phil *Shankly* Bluecoat Press (1993)
Toshack, John *Tosh – an Autobiography* Arthur Barker (1982)
Walmsley, David and Done, Stephen *The Treasures of Liverpool FC* Carlton (2004)
Yeats, Ron *Soccer with a Mersey Beat* Pelham (1966)

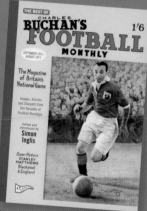
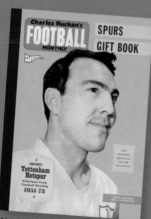
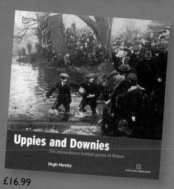

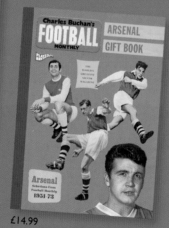